ROUTLEDGE LIBRARY EDITIONS: WELFARE AND THE STATE

Volume 3

SOCIAL SECURITY AND SOCIETY

SOCIAL SECURITY AND SOCIETY

VICTOR GEORGE

Routledge
Taylor & Francis Group

LONDON AND NEW YORK

First published in 1973 by Routledge and Kegan Paul Ltd.

This edition first published in 2019
by Routledge
2 Park Square, Milton Park, Abingdon, Oxon OX14 4RN

and by Routledge
711 Third Avenue, New York, NY 10017

Routledge is an imprint of the Taylor & Francis Group, an informa business

© 1973 Victor George

British Library Cataloguing in Publication Data
A catalogue record for this book is available from the British Library

ISBN: 978-1-138-61373-7 (Set)
ISBN: 978-0-429-45813-2 (Set) (ebk)
ISBN: 978-1-138-60060-7 (Volume 3) (hbk)
ISBN: 978-1-138-60061-4 (Volume 3) (pbk)
ISBN: 978-0-429-47082-0 (Volume 3) (ebk)

Publisher's Note
The publisher has gone to great lengths to ensure the quality of this reprint but points out that some imperfections in the original copies may be apparent.

Disclaimer
The publisher has made every effort to trace copyright holders and would welcome correspondence from those they have been unable to trace.

Social security and society

Victor George

Department of Applied Social Science
University of Nottingham

Routledge & Kegan Paul
LONDON AND BOSTON

First published in 1973
by Routledge & Kegan Paul Ltd
Broadway House, 68–74 Carter Lane,
London EC4V 5EL and
9 Park Street,
Boston, Mass. 02108, U.S.A.

Printed in Great Britain by
Unwin Brothers Limited
The Gresham Press, Old Woking, Surrey

ISBN 0 7100 7642 8 (c)
ISBN 0 7100 7643 6 (p)

Library of Congress Catalog Card No. 73–79110

Contents

Tables

∽∽∽∽∽∽∽∽∽∽∽∽∽∽∽
Acknowledgments
∽∽∽∽∽∽∽∽∽∽∽∽∽∽∽

The central theme of this book is that social class conflict has played a very dominant part in the formulation of social security. This conflict has at times been open and at other times concealed under the cloak of ideological consensus. This relationship between social class conflict and social security has, however, been a two-way process. Social security is an integral part of society—it is influenced by other institutions and forces in society and it influences them in return.

In a book of this kind one owes a debt to many people. I feel especially indebted, however, to two colleagues and friends, Paul Wilding and Richard Silburn, who have read the book in draft and have made useful suggestions. My greatest debt is to my wife whose help and encouragement have been most valuable and who also typed the manuscript several times.

Since this is a personal viewpoint of social security, it may be worth mentioning that I alone am responsible for everything which appears in this book.

I

〜〜〜〜〜〜〜〜〜〜〜〜〜〜〜〜〜

The development
of social security and
the ruling classes

〜〜〜〜〜〜〜〜〜〜〜〜〜〜〜〜〜

Our historical discussion of the development of social security services will be along two inter-related lines: how the understanding of the problem of poverty has changed over the years and how, despite these changes, the strongest continuing influence in the development of the social security system has been the successful attempt of the dominant social groups to buttress the existing social and economic order.

The problem of poverty has been seen in four different ways, each reflecting the type of society in which it existed: poverty as an ascribed status in feudal societies; poverty as vagabondage in the immediate aftermath of the collapse of feudalism; as an individual problem of physical subsistence attributable to the individual's personal failings from the mid-seventeenth to the beginning of the present century; and finally as a social problem of physical subsistence and social inequality during this century. A problem is defined as social instead of a collection of individual problems if it is accepted that its causes are to be found in the social and economic structure of society and therefore needing government action to change those aspects of the socio-economic structure that give rise to it.[1] Many social problems are primarily issues involving conflict of economic interests between the various social classes in society. None of these four stages in the development of the concept of poverty breaks cleanly from the one which precedes or succeeds it. They are ideal types which dominate during a certain period and they merge gradually and can therefore co-exist with the stage immediately before and after them.

The suggestion that government policies for poverty have safeguarded the interests of the ruling classes does not deny that these policies also benefited some groups of the poor in varying degrees. It merely claims that the benefits they provided for the poor were either negligible or not inconsistent with the interests of the wealthy or both. In general there has been a historical movement away from policies that discriminate and stigmatize the

I

poor in a blatant way towards policies which try to conciliate and build bridges between the dominated and the dominant groups in society. This trend started at the beginning of this century and its effects have mainly been to reduce the intensity of social class conflict even if the gap between the working class and the upper class in terms of economic power has not changed.

The central theme that runs through our historical discussion is that there exists in society a constant conflict between the social classes in economic affairs which is reflected in government policies on poverty.[2] The model of the social system, in other words, we have adopted is one of conflict of interests rather than consensus of values and interests between the two vaguely defined groups in society, the working class which includes the poor and the upper class which includes the ruling class. These two classes have possessed unequal power with the result that the upper classes have been able to resolve conflict situations to their advantage. There is nothing unnatural in this since the dominant social values have always stressed individualism and individual profit.

Three main methods have been used by the upper classes to resolve conflicts to their benefit. First, the use of force or the threat of the use of force by the government against individuals or groups who have threatened or questioned seriously the nature of the existing social order. Power, however, has to be applied sparingly and strategically by the ruling classes if it is not to evoke united and concerted opposition from the working class which after all constitutes the largest social group. Thus there is the need for a less oppressive and a less obvious form of control-authority. This is the creation of ideologies which serve the economic interests of the ruling classes and the securing of the acceptance of such class ideologies as 'national' ideologies serving the interests of all sections of the community. Once such class ideologies are accepted by the working class as national, they are obeyed and the need for coercive measures to preserve the *status quo* diminishes. In other words the subordinate members of a group in a conflict situation come to 'control themselves as much as they are controlled by others'.[3] Third, the process of assimilation whereby leaders of radical movements or parties are absorbed into the way of life of the ruling classes with the obvious detrimental results on the interests of the working class. The working of these three methods will be illustrated in the discussion that follows where it will become clear that there has been a trend away from open, ruthless forms of coercion towards the other two forms of social control which are more subtle, less obvious and more difficult to substantiate but nevertheless equally effective.[4]

Poverty in feudal society

In the rigidly stratified feudal society, poverty was not considered a social problem. One was born poor or rich and was definitely destined to remain so for the rest of his life. In other words, wealth and poverty were ascribed statuses that could not be altered. A condition which is considered natural and unalterable cannot at the same time be viewed as a social problem for this implies a recognition that something is wrong and that government action should be used to solve or at least ameliorate the situation.

Not only was poverty not seen as a social problem but on the contrary it was idealized, considered in positive terms. Life on this earth, according to the early teachings of the Church, was a prelude and a preparation for the important business of life after death. Poverty was an advantage for it was considered far easier for the poor than for the wealthy to gain salvation in life after death. To be born poor was almost to be born lucky.

Poverty had another useful function—to provide opportunities for the wealthy to prove that they observed the Christian teaching of giving alms and doing good deeds to the poor. Without such conduct, the rich could not expect to enter paradise. In other words, 'Giving alms was meant to increase the chances of the giver in the next world and not primarily to improve the chances of the poor in this'.[5] The funerals of important persons were sometimes used as occasions for giving alms to the poor as a last parting gesture by the deceased to the Almighty.

Thus the social and religious ideology of the period plus the fact that the nobility were the government as well as the possessors of wealth, ensured that the poor were content with their lot or if they were not, they did not express it in any way that challenged the established social order. It may well be true that the serfs were well fed and that it was only when crops failed that they starved and even then their lords also suffered. Jordan[6] argues that the economy of the Middle Ages 'was perennially vulnerable to poverty occasioned by local disaster, with the consequence that, if the serf died, his lord had at least gone very hungry and so had his parish priest'. This does not alter the fact that through force and religious and social indoctrination, the serfs and the lords

3

considered their status in society as natural and unalterable with the result that wealth and poverty were considered also as natural and unalterable conditions in life.

The transition period: 1350–1601

The growth of woollen manufactures, the changes of land from cultivation to pastures for sheep, the growth of commerce with foreign countries, the wars in France, the Black Death and other economic and social changes brought about the gradual collapse of the feudal system. By the middle of the fourteenth century, feudalism as a social, political and economic system had largely disappeared. Mobility of the population became possible, wages came to be the accepted method of contract between employer and worker and the freedom of the individual in theory, if not in practice, replaced the servility of the serf to his lord. A new class of poor was created—'the dispossessed, the masterless and the incompetent' who 'were literally set in motion by irresistible forces as they sought first work that was not to be had and then alms which society was neither equipped nor disposed to give'.[7] This was at a time when the nobility began to feel less responsible for the relief of their serfs for they had no such responsibility in theory. The government, what existed of it apart from individual nobles, did not consider the relief of the poor as its responsibility either and looked to the Church to assume this role. Monasteries, churches, hospitals and other institutions run by the Church became the national network for relieving poverty. Their responsibility, however, was a moral and not a contractual one as that which existed between serfs and nobles. In practice what this meant was that whereas under feudalism serfs starved or died when crops failed, now they could suffer the same fate if they were unemployed, whatever the state of the harvest was. When they were employed, of course, they could enjoy a standard of living above that of the serfs. Their life chances were now more unpredictable; there was more hope as well as more despair in the free economy and society.

Poverty was still not considered as a social problem during this period. What the government considered as a social problem was the influx of large numbers of poor people in the towns who were unemployed and in search of relief or alms. They were seen as a threat to the existing social order, they were branded with various labels—vagabonds, rogues, etc.—and they became the legitimate target of government coercive and repressive measures. The government saw its role as keeping the peace, preserving the *status quo* rather than providing employment or relieving poverty. Thus the legislation of the fifteenth and the first half of the sixteenth century was predominantly repressive designed to reduce population mobility and to punish begging and vagrancy. Much of the legislation of this period 'was aimed at vagrancy and the disorders accompanying it tending to assume that poverty and vagrancy were synonymous. The notion persisted that hungry men were invincibly idle men, that poverty was a consequence of moral fault.'[8] Poverty in other words became equated with laziness, crime and with subversive behaviour which the state felt ought to be mercilessly repressed. This is an early example of the state resorting to open repression of the poor when the gentler forms of persuasion and ideological indoctrination failed.

The history of poor relief was given an unexpected twist in the early part of the sixteenth century when Henry VIII confiscated the property of the monasteries and the Church. At a time when the number of the unemployed poor was rising, the major relieving agencies were impoverished. The result was a worsening of an already acute problem at least for a few decades until the government found some other agency to carry out poor relief. This new agency was the local parish. At first the wealthy members of the parish were asked to help the poor that lived in their midst on a voluntary basis; when exhortation failed, compulsion was introduced during the last quarter of the sixteenth century. The various Acts of the last quarter of the sixteenth century were incorporated and enlarged in the Elizabethan Act of 1601 which came to guide poor relief for over two centuries. It is always difficult to be certain about the motives of legislators but opinion is fairly unanimous that one of the main—if not the main—motives of the monarchy for introducing less ruthless policy measures for the relief of poverty was to avert serious political unrest among the agrarian population that suffered as a result of the agrarian changes. 'It may safely be said,' to quote Jordan again, 'that the steady concern of the Tudors with the problem of poverty flowed from the almost obsessive preoccupation of these greater rulers with the question of public order.' They were 'deeply persuaded that unrelieved and uncontrolled poverty was the most fertile breeding ground for local disasters which might by a kind of social contagion flame across the whole realm'.[9] Rimlinger in a comparative study takes a very similar view:[10] 'In England, France and other European countries, governments became initially concerned with the lot of the poor not for purposes of relieving suffering, but for the maintenance of law and order.'

The parish relief system: 1601–1834

The Elizabethan Act required parishes to provide relief to their poor out of taxes compulsorily levied on their wealthier members. The massive repression of previous centuries had proved unsuccessful in dealing with the problem of poverty and this Act and the legislation which it incorporated marked in theory a departure from the past in that it suggested reform for the deserving poor and punishment for the undeserving. The ruling classes of that period and long afterwards believed not only that they had a natural right to discipline and to reform the poor but that they had also a natural gift for it. Apart from the fact that the distinction between deserving and undeserving poor is false, it was cheaper and easier to punish than to reform people. The Civil War made matters worse because of the obvious anarchy it created which resulted in the collapse of the administrative system on a local basis and more important of the central government machinery that was designed to ensure that parishes complied with the requirements of the Act. The result was that apart from a few years immediately after the Act was passed, repression became once again the dominant feature of the poor law system.

Before we look at the methods of poor relief adopted during the second half of the seventeenth and the eighteenth centuries, it is necessary to understand the dominant philosophy regarding the nature of poverty of this period. This was a period of commercial and industrial expansion, of the building of the Empire and of increasing prosperity for the emerging middle class. It was felt that there was work for all that genuinely wanted it and that if people were poor it was because they were lazy either through some inborn characteristic or through custom and habit. Since so many people were poor, the working class was considered generally as being idle. To make them work, one had to be strict with them. Wages should be kept low to force people to remain at work all the time. If they were high, people would work far less because lazy people work not because they want to but because they have to. As the contemporary writer, Arthur Young, wrote: 'Everyone but an idiot knows that the lower classes must be kept poor or they will never be industrious.' In Tawney's opinion,[11] Young's verdict was not isolated but it 'was the tritest commonplace of Restoration economists. It was not argued; it was accepted as self-evident.'

This lay view of poverty was reinforced by the new religious view of the nature of work—the Calvinist, protestant ethic as it has come to be known. According to this view, being out of work or not working hard enough when employed was a sin because it was a waste of God's time. People are on this earth by the grace of God for a number of years and they should use their allocated time to the full. To work hard, to lead an austere life and to save one's money became part of the Christian way of life. Material possessions were a sign of moral excellence, a fulfilment of God's will. It was thus inevitable that 'A society which reverences the attainment of riches as the supreme felicity will naturally be disposed to regard the poor as damned in the next world, if only to justify itself for making their life a hell in this.'[12] Whatever else it may have been, this was a doctrine that was clearly favourable to industrial and commercial expansion.

These two views of poverty and of work meant that the poor were not only idle but sinners as well. Poverty was not seen as the result of forces within the social structure of society but as the result of the individual's decision whether to work or not. Poverty was in other words a personal problem for the individuals concerned and not a social problem for society. The solution to the problem did not lie in government social policies to provide employment opportunities, to safeguard wages, etc., but in the individuals themselves. If only they changed their idle nature, they would at the same time solve their problem of being poor.

Overriding these views on the nature of poverty and work was the new theory regarding the relationship between the government and the citizen. All through feudal times, during this period and down to the beginning of the twentieth century, the government and the other parts of the state like the judiciary, the civil service, etc., were directly controlled and run by the ruling classes. 'Government was not by the people, and along its main lines there was little pretence of its being for them. Its duty was not to them but theirs to it.'[13] During feudal times, the ruling class, which was also the government, felt a certain moral obligation towards the poor. It was a paternalistic attitude reflecting social relationships of a rigidly stratified society. The collapse of feudalism meant that a new relationship between the ruling class and the working class was necessary. The French Revolution provided one answer —the state should serve the interests of the people; British Liberalism provided another—the principles of individualism and *laissez-faire*. British writers of this period—Townsend, Malthus,

Adam Smith and others—argued that the individual must be free to pursue his own welfare as he pleases. Every individual must be master of his own fate, responsible for his actions, free to pursue policies that suit him best. What is good for the individual is good for society as a whole, for society is nothing more than a collectivity of free individuals. The government can best help each individual and society in general by providing an administrative framework that encouraged free competition among individuals, even if the competition was between unequal persons or groups. Excessive government intervention undermines individualism and thus it causes harm to the welfare of individuals and to society as a whole. The twin principles of *laissez-faire* were clearly to the advantage of the ruling class for it allowed industrialists a free hand to pursue policies that maximised profits irrespective of the human consequences. If people worked long hours, in unsuitable conditions, were paid low wages, and so on, it was not considered to be the concern of the government. The important thing was that each individual was free to do as he pleased even if this theoretical independence was utterly meaningless to the mass of the people and even if it meant starvation, hardship and exploitation to many of them. Conducive as the doctrine of individualism was for industrialization and the immediate interests of the ruling class, it contained the seeds of future discontent. If the working class was expected to be self-dependent what was to stop it eventually from demanding equality in political power? If the ruling class disclaimed any paternalistic duty to support the poor, how was it to justify its superior position in society?

These views on poverty, on work and on the place of state action in society were supported, it was argued, by statistical evidence which showed that though the amount of money spent on poor relief had increased, the number of poor and destitute had also increased. The inference was drawn that the more the parishes spent on poor relief, the more they undermined people's willingness and ability to work and support themselves and their families. 'The evil was held to emanate from the relief rather than from the situation, which was the occasion of relief.'[14] For some the only real answer to the problem was the abolition of poor relief altogether while for others it was to make the life of those on poor relief as difficult as possible by paying as little as possible and by making the receipt of relief as humiliating as possible. These views on poor relief developed through the seventeenth and eighteenth centuries and they affected the system of poor relief not only then but also all through the nineteenth century. It is not surprising, therefore, to find that social policy for poverty during this period was repressive and punitive. Apart from outdoor relief, three main methods were employed by the parishes to deal with poverty: the workhouse, the Roundsman system and the Speenhamland system.

A few workhouses existed in the main cities before the eighteenth century. It was, however, the Act of 1722 that provided the impetus for the provision of workhouses on a large scale in the country. What was new was not the provision of residential care for the poor but the philosophy behind this new drive for workhouses. The parish overseers were authorized to refuse relief to anyone unless he and his family were willing to enter the workhouse. Life in the workhouse was intentionally made harsh both as regards the standard of living and the discipline to deter people from it. To make matters worse parishes were authorized to contract the workhouse out to businessmen who were willing to run it and care for the poor for a fee. Inevitably this meant the lowest form of life in the workhouse since both the parish and the contractor were interested in saving and making money out of the transaction. Moreover, workhouses were used for all age groups, for both sexes, for people of all marital statuses and backgrounds. They were mixed, general workhouses run on the philosophy of punishment and deterrence. They were very different from the few workhouses that existed at the end of the seventeenth century whose aims were to provide employment, to train and to rehabilitate the poor and the unemployed. This turn to harshness was the result of the emerging theories on the nature of poverty and work we discussed. For the upper classes it meant a cheap and plentiful supply of labour. For the working class it meant the unenviable choice between refusing to go into the workhouse and therefore starve, or entering the workhouse and leading a life of semi-starvation and humiliation.

Unemployment and poverty continued to grow in spite of the severity of the workhouse. This was particularly true of the rural areas for the economic changes of the eighteenth century affected them most. These changes were the decline in the family industry of spinning and weaving and the enclosure movement. 'In the very years in which Revolution was restoring the fields of France to its peasantry, England was developing a landed aristocracy and creating a landless poor.'[15] The doctrine of individualism dictated that unemployed rural workers should use their initiative and

9

move to the towns for employment in the new industries. Many, of course, did but many did not and for these the same doctrine approved of poor relief at the minimum possible level. Since workhouses were not so prevalent in rural areas other methods of relief had to be used. Hence the Roundsman and the Speenhamland system sometimes used jointly and at other times separately. The Roundsman system was 'a sort of billeting of the unemployed labour upon the parishioners in rotation, each in turn having to provide maintenance and being free to exact service.'[16] The Speenhamland system meant that a labourer's wages were supplemented out of parish funds up to a certain level depending on the number of children he had to support. It was adopted in preference to a plan for a minimum wage for a number of reasons. In the first place it gave the parish authorities full control over the lives of unemployed or low paid workers. The parish authorities could decide to grant the unemployed outdoor relief without any conditions or they could farm him out to a willing or unwilling local employer who would pay what wages he could or would with the parish paying what supplement was necessary. In the second place it spread the financial burden to all the parishioners instead of placing it on the large landowners who were the main employers of farm labour. The rich landowners were the ruling power group within the parish and clearly preferred supplementation of wages to a system of a minimum wage in spite of the fact that legislation for minimum and maximum wages had been used several times in the past in the country. Nevertheless, the Speenhamland system was not only a welcome respite from the oppressive life of the workhouses but it also ensured that workers and their families did not starve whatever the economic conditions were. Whatever the reasons for the introduction of the Speenhamland and the Roundsman systems, their perpetuation was ensured for a time 'by the demand of the larger farmers—in an industry which has exceptional requirements for occasional or casual labour—for a permanent cheap labour reserve'.[17] It made possible the payment of starvation wages irrespective of the worker's effort or trade since 'both the Parish authorities and the employers could screw down the rates *and* wages actually paid out because the other would make up whatever was needed in order to provide the minimum provided by law'.[18]

At a period when the working class had no clear political power and the trade unions were not in existence, the Speenhamland system made the unemployed worker the property of the parish authorities, it held back any improvement in wages and naturally it led to a rise in public expenditure on poor relief. It was this last effect—the rise in expenditure on poor relief—that went contrary to the doctrines of *laissez-faire* and individualism for it not only reflected the fact that an increasing number of people had to rely partly or wholly on parish relief but it also provided the 'evidence'—dubious though it was—that parish relief undermined people's willingness to fend for themselves. The ruling class rejected the idea of a minimum wage, resented the rise in public expenditure on poor relief and demanded the use of the deterrent workhouse on more systematic lines not only in the urban but in the rural areas as well. It failed or refused to recognize that poverty was the fault of the economic system and by so doing it delayed any rational policies for the solution of the problem for another century. The workhouse principles of 1722 were applied with greater uniformity, with harsher severity and on a larger scale after the Poor Law Act, 1834. This return to increased oppression of the poor became politically possible as a result of the alliance between the emerging middle class and the established upper class. The effects of the French Revolution on radicals in this country were slight and short-lived largely because the upper class had begun to accommodate among its ranks members of the wealthy middle class. It is true that the aristocracy's acceptance of the new industrial class was reluctant and half-hearted. It is also true that though men of the new industrial class were anxious to receive the status of aristocracy they did not feel at home in their new status for many of them had not outgrown their proletarian peasant background. Nevertheless, as Tawney has remarked,[19]

> Men do not burn down the house which they intend to occupy, even though they regard its existing tenant as a public nuisance. The characteristic features which distinguished the social life of England from that of France— the small part played by legal privilege, the public duties discharged by the landed gentry, the immensely greater importance of manufactures and commerce as compared with agriculture, the fact that the small property-owners were declining in number while the wage-workers were growing— all combined to muffle the tones in which the middle classes denounced the oligarchy, lest they should prove too effective in exciting the populace.

1834–1911 period

The Poor Law Act of 1834, introduced no new principles. It re-affirmed the two deterrent principles of previous legislation—the workhouse test and the doctrine of less eligibility. What is distinctive about this legislation, is first, that for the first time the central government intervened to direct and to supervize closely the work of local authorities through the Poor Law Board and its inspectors; and second, the strong moral arguments that were used to justify the harshness of the system. As Schweinitz has said,[20] the Poor Law Act 'was more than an ordinary document of state. It was a pronouncement as it were from Sinai. It established what was almost in the nature of a moral code. It was a doctrine founded in statute.' The doctrine of less eligibility was given its classical definition and has since become the ghost haunting many a well-intentioned piece of social reform. 'The first and most essential of all conditions,' declared the Poor Law Commissioners, 'is that the situation of the individual relieved shall not be made really or apparently so eligible as the situation of the independent labourer of the lowest class.' This was necessary for the 'national interest' because 'we do not believe that a country in which that distinction has been completely effaced, and every man, whatever be his conduct or his character, ensured a comfortable subsistence, can retain its prosperity, or even its civilization.'[21] It was this singlemindedness of the Poor Law Act that provoked even Disraeli to remark that it 'announces to the world that in England poverty is a crime'.[22]

The 1834 Act is relevant to our discussion from the additional point of view that it illustrates the process of legitimation of ruling class values to national values. The Act was preceded by a long campaign of indoctrination seeking to popularize the notion that individualism and wealth were associated with morality while dependency and poverty were synonymous with immorality. Malthus's views that poor relief was a bounty on population was being increasingly accepted and moreover was increasingly seen, in the words of the Poor Law Commissioners of 1834, as 'a bounty on indolence and vice'. In other words the views we discussed earlier that were conducive to industrialization had gradually gained general public acceptance. The massive researches which preceded the 1834 Act were variously manipulated to prove that liberal out-door relief was a disaster to the individual and to the nation and that the harsh, deterrent workhouse relief was the only real solution to the problem of poverty. In McGregor's words, [23] 'Of all the empirical investigations before the fifties that which preceded the Act of 1834 was the least open-minded, the most concerned to validate the presuppositions of political economy.' Thus social values which were clearly to the economic advantage of the upper classes became accepted as national social values. They justified a punitive system of poor relief and through it the injustices of the industrial system.

> Long hours, poor health conditions, cruel exploitation of children, low wages, and all similar conditions could be explained or justified, if need be, if the source of all misery was the improvidence of the laboring people, as the New Poor Law seemed to imply. Though not intended for this purpose, the 'well-managed work-house' appeared to give added justification to the manufacturers' exercise of iron discipline in their industries. [24]

The second half of the nineteenth century is vital to our discussion because it was during this period that the campaign for social reform became strong enough to force the higher classes into action. There were two primary and three secondary factors, all inter-related in one way or another, for this upsurge of public demand for government intervention to protect the economic interests of the poor. The enfranchisement of the working class and the spread of socialist ideas were the two primary factors. The right to vote was granted to the working class in 1867–85 and from then on governments could not afford to ignore all demands for social reform blatantly and indefinitely. As Gilbert has stated, [25] 'The Poor Law . . . treated an applicant for relief as a quasi-criminal and sought to force him by the pressure of humiliation and discipline back into the labour market. So long as the men who made the laws were not elected by the people who were likely to become clients of the Poor Law such a system could work.' Now that their election to government office depended on the votes of the working class, politicians, sooner or later, had to be seen as attempting to solve the problem of poverty and other problems if they wanted to stay in office. On the other hand, however, both the Conservative and Liberal governments represented the interests of the ruling class and the solutions they proposed or they accepted could not have been radical enough to undermine its economic interests. The formation of the Labour Party at the end of the nineteenth century and the election of working-class candidates as Members of Parliament were a clear warning to the Conservative and Liberal parties of what could happen if the working class acted in solidarity. Discussing the British experience, Rimlinger[26] concludes that 'to a large extent social security emerged as part of a contest among the major political parties of the country for the support of the enfranchised working classes'.

The spread of socialist ideas and particularly of revolutionary Marxism provided the working class with the unifying class consciousness that was indispensable not only for the formulation of programmes of reform but also for the growth of the determination to use political and industrial power to back up the demands for reform. The marches, protests and riots of workers in London during the last quarter of the century were signs that the working class was determined to achieve reforms even if it were divided on the kind of reforms it wanted. Gilbert goes as far as to claim that though there had been workers' riots before, particularly in the 1830s and 1840s, they were of a different nature.

> Then the mobs' anger had been directed at particular individuals, at the reactionary politicians who all men of good and liberal minds could likewise denounce. Now the attack was on the established order itself, directed not at individuals but at property. To satisfy the poor, the rich could do nothing but give up their wealth.[27]

The aim of the rioters now was not only to replace the individuals in authority but to change the political system itself. It would be a mistake to consider the revolutionary spirit of this period as the only driving force behind social reform for the working class was divided in its aims and in the means it was prepared to use to achieve its aims. On the other hand it would be unrealistic to underestimate the effects of revolutionary ideas and practices on the process of social reform.

The three secondary factors of the movement for social reform were the paternalistic humanitarianism of this period, the realization that the amelioration of poverty paid economic dividends to industrialists and the social surveys that quantified the extent and causes of poverty. The humanitarianism of the period reflected largely the guilty feelings of some of the affluent intellectuals and professionals who could not justify the existence of starvation and poverty in the middle of obvious and increasing wealth. Beatrice Webb[28] referred to this feeling as the 'consciousness of sin' which she defined as 'a collective or class consciousness, a growing uneasiness, amounting to conviction, that the industrial organization which had yielded rent, interest and profits on a stupendous scale, had failed to provide a decent livelihood and tolerable conditions for a majority of the inhabitants of Great Britain'. The humanitarian response was partly moral and partly religious. It was not poverty as such but the immorality that could flow from it that haunted the religious philanthropists. They were not so much concerned with the effects of poverty on the well-being of the poor in this world but rather with its repercussions on life after death. Whether motivated by moral or by religious ideas, the philanthropists' aim was not to replace the existing economic and political system with something substantially different but to modify it, to remove its glaring injustices.

By the end of the nineteenth century, the industrial expansion of the country became increasingly dependent on a labour force that was skilled, efficient and co-operative with management. Starting with Robert Owen, a few industrialists came to realize that the payment of a living wage or of adequate poor relief or the provision of education and health services were not a threat but an asset to the economic prosperity of industry. The development of personnel and welfare departments in industry were the outcome of this realization. 'Protection of the worker from want and worry thus became an economically rational (profit-oriented) activity.'[29] Limited social reform in this view would improve the standard of living of everybody and at the same time leave untouched the extent of economic inequality.

Finally the social surveys of Booth and Rowntree in London and in York in the 1880s provided statistical evidence first that poverty was widespread and second that, on the whole, it was not the result of the character deficiencies of the individuals concerned but of the economic system in which they lived. Poverty was not simply a problem for the individuals affected but for society—it was not an individual but a social problem. 'Booth's importance,' writes Gilbert,[30] 'lay in bringing home to the mass of thinking Englishmen the fact that the relief of distress, because of the sheer numbers involved, could not be the relief of individuals.' Without belittling the contribution of Rowntree and Booth to the recognition of poverty as a social problem demanding social action, it must be pointed out that previous surveys, perhaps not so rigorous, both government and private, had shown the wide prevalence of poverty. What changed, however, was the political and social climate in the country that made its leadership more open-minded and willing to consider and to understand the meaning of the new data on poverty. Facts do not always speak for themselves. They have first to be acknowledged, then to be interpreted and the interpretation that becomes acceptable for social action, if any, depends on the prevailing political situation.

As a result of all these pressures, poverty was beginning to be recognized as a social problem which had its roots in the economic structure of society and which could only be solved if the institutional factors in the economic system that gave rise to it were dealt with by government action. The scene was set for a protracted conflict between the working class and the upper classes. Partial solutions to the problem in the form of accommodations and compromises were found reflecting the divisions of opinion within the various classes in the country. This division of opinion was partly reflected in the fact that the Royal Commission on the Poor Law appointed in 1905 produced a Majority and a Minority Report four years later. The unanimity and singlemindedness which characterized the report of 1834 on the workhouse test and the principle of less eligibility had given way to confusion and vagueness. There was now less emphasis on deterrence though not complete abandonment of the principle; there was more emphasis on treatment and help to those in need but always qualified so as not to undermine the virtues of self-help and independence; there was less emphasis on forcing people into the workhouse, though not complete abolition of the workhouses.

The social policy measures seriously discussed and those which were introduced during the years before the outbreak of the First World War had one feature in common. They did not represent an attack, let alone a threat, to the economic position of the ruling class. They did not aim at replacing the capitalist system but at making it more humane and more efficient. In the field of social security two Acts were passed—the Old Age Pensions Act, 1908, and the National Insurance Act, 1911—which represented slightly different philosophies on social policy. Both Acts also reflect the conflict in values and attitudes that existed between the reformers and the supporters of the *status quo*. The Old Age Pensions Act was potentially more of a socialist measure than the National Insurance Act. It provided a pension of five shillings a week to old people who were seventy years old or more. Yet to satisfy the demands of the 'conservatives' it made the payment of the income conditional on an income test. Those whose income exceeded the stipulated maximum received no pension, those whose income was below the minimum received the full pension and those whose income was between the maximum and minimum received a part of the pension. Secondly, a number of moral clauses were included in the Act which disqualified a number of people whose previous life had not been morally correct—they had not worked regularly, they had been convicted of drunkenness, etc. The inevitable result was that old age pensions retained some of the stigma of poor relief. Without the income test and the moral clauses this Act could have been a model of socialist legislation in social security for it would have provided a pension to all, irrespective of their economic or other background. Since it was financed out of government funds it would have also involved some vertical redistribution of income.

It was, however, the National Insurance Act, 1911, that proved the most important piece of legislation during this period for it determined the nature of future social security legislation in this country. This Act required people at work to pay contributions which entitled them to a benefit when they were out of work because of illness or unemployment. Employers and the State contributed to the fund which financed the benefits. The Act covered most manual workers in case of illness but only a small section of the unemployed. Those in non-manual occupations were excluded unless their income was below a certain amount. People paid flat rate contributions and received flat rate benefits. Those who had not paid any contributions or who had not paid the minimum number of contributions were not entitled to any benefits. Health insurance was administered by approved non-profit societies that were part of friendly insurance societies or of commercial insurance companies or of trade unions. Unemployment was administered mainly by the new government system of employment exchanges.

The insurance principle was very much in line with middle- and upper-class values on individualism and self-help. We already saw how the value of individualism was transformed from an upper-class value to a national value during the latter part of the eighteenth century. The same process can be observed for the value of self-help. Bendix argues that the value of self-help, through the works of Samuel Smiles in the second half of the nineteenth century, was used by the upper classes to help legitimize their authority over the working class in the new industrial and political climate of the period. The doctrine of self-help gave hope

17

to the workers for it announced that they, too, could become rich and powerful in the same way that some of their industrial bosses had. It 'proclaimed that employers and workers were alike in self-dependence, and that regardless of class each man's success was a proof of himself and a contribution to the common wealth'.[31] In this way workers were more likely to accept the position of the upper classes as legitimate and to try to emulate them.

Self-help is functional to the growth of industrialization and to the economic interests of the upper classes in another way. It requires people to make savings which can be used to expand industries and which can prevent a person relying on the State for help. While saving is not such a sacrifice for those with good incomes it is near impossible for the lower paid. Moreover, while large savings when invested in a businesslike way can produce worthwhile profit, small savings cannot be of much economic value. The harshness of the Poor Law forced many workers to take out insurance policies against sickness, unemployment and other such risks with friendly societies or trade unions. These were mainly skilled workers with fairly stable jobs and regular wages. Insurance, however, came to be seen as the respectable, the sensible way to make provision for one's financial problems. Thus from a middle-class practice based on middle-class values, it spread to the stable working-class section and the Insurance Act, 1911, extended it into a national practice based on a national social value. Insurance was proclaimed to be in the interests of the individual and of the nation as a whole. It was in a sense a compromise solution between those who felt that the state should be fully responsible for the welfare of its citizens and those who still argued that the individual is responsible for his own welfare. Collective action through the state and individual responsibility were harnessed together in an economic alliance that presented no threat to the economic position of the ruling class.

The motives behind the provision of insurance benefits 'can hardly be described as philanthropic. National insurance was the Liberal response to the threat of socialism.'[32] In the first place it was felt that the National Insurance Act would help to undermine the growth of a revolutionary Marxist movement in the country. Contented workers are not a real threat to the social system even if they do not accept it fully. Britain was copying the example of Bismarck's Germany which was the first European country to introduce insurance schemes 'out of fear that the prevailing social order might be overthrown by revolutionary agitation of the working class'.[33] Though the official leadership of the Labour Party accepted the insurance principle, a substantial section of the party, mainly the left wing, were against it.[34] Second, it placed most of the financial burden on the workers. Since contributions were of a flat rate nature, they weighed more heavily on the lower paid workers—they were a regressive form of taxation. Third, the fact that the employers and the state contributed towards the cost of the benefits was seen as evidence of the cohesion and integration of the British society—one nation with no gaps between the classes that were unbridgeable. As Rimlinger has concluded,[35] 'To the extent that those who might become poor were forced to protect themselves from want, society as a whole, but particularly the rich, was protected from the poor. In this sense, social insurance has become an important form of protection for the rich.'

Undoubtedly, however, insurance benefits were a vast improvement over poor relief and this explains their widespread acceptance by the public at the time and since. Insurance benefits protected the self-respect of the unemployed and the sick from the humiliating means test of the Poor Law system; and they provided a floor on which the unemployed and the sick could add any other income they had for insurance benefits were paid irrespective of the financial position of the recipient. National insurance was a financial transaction involving no attempt to reform or to punish the person who received the benefit. On the other hand it did not place a heavy financial burden on the rich nor did it attempt to change the economic system in favour of a more egalitarian society. It is an excellent example of a social policy measure widely acclaimed as a radical departure from past practice but which not only leaves the economic supremacy of the ruling class intact but which also makes its position in society more secure.

1914–1948 period

The period between the wars provided no major innovation in the field of social security. The insurance principle became generally accepted as the best method for providing benefits. The sickness and the unemployment insurance schemes of 1911 were extended so that by the outbreak of the Second World War they covered most of the working-class population. A new insurance scheme was introduced in 1925 to provide widows' benefits and old age pensions financed out of contributions instead of taxation as was the case for the first old age pension scheme of 1908.

The mass unemployment of the thirties showed up the weaknesses of the unemployment insurance scheme and led to important administrative changes. Unemployment benefit was paid for a period of six months only on the assumption that the unemployed person would be able to find a new job within that period. The mass unemployment of the thirties, however, meant that most people could not find a job within six months with the result that thousands of the unemployed had to rely on poor relief paid after a means test by the local authorities. Apart from the general dislike of the means test this meant that those local authorities with the highest rates of unemployment had to pay out the largest sums in poor relief for the unemployed. This had always been the case but the sheer numbers involved in the thirties highlighted the undesirability of such a scheme. The central government was forced to accept the responsibility for the relief of the unemployed and created the Unemployment Assistance Board in 1934 to be responsible for the administration of assistance to the unemployed for the whole country. The functions of this Board were extended during the war and in 1948 it became responsible for the payment of national assistance, as it became known, for all people in need for the whole country. In this way the local authorities which from 1601 were responsible for poor relief in their boundaries gave way to a national body responsible for assistance for the whole country. It was not an administrative change only but a change involving substantial improvements in the ways in which the means test was interpreted and applied.

The mass unemployment of the thirties also provided the evidence, if any was needed, that social security benefits for controllable risks are only meaningful if a serious attempt is made by the government to abolish or reduce these risks. Schemes for unemployment benefits or sickness benefits or disability can only function and thus make sense only if the government provides services to control the extent of unemployment, sickness and accidents in society.

The inter-war period is of vital importance to the concept of the welfare state first because it witnessed the emergence of the first Labour government, briefly in 1924 and for eighteen months between 1929 and 1931; and secondly because it produced the most serious challenge to the ruling class in the form of the General Strike of 1926. The two Labour governments not only did not attempt any fundamental changes to the social security system but also showed that their aims were not substantially different from those of the Conservative Party or the declining Liberal Party.

The Labour Party both in opposition and in power made it clear that it was not opposed to the capitalist system as such but rather to the inhuman and unreformed type of capitalism that existed in this country at that time. The Labour Party became the strongest advocate of a reformed capitalist system which would include full employment, regular wages and a wide range of social services. Its election manifesto of 1922 made this and much more quite clear.[36] 'Democratic government can be made effective in this country,' it declared, 'without bloodshed or violence. Labour's policy is to bring about a more equitable distribution of the nation's wealth by constitutional means.' It concluded that 'This is neither Bolshevism nor Communism, but common sense and justice. This is Labour's alternative to Reaction and Revolution.' The Labour Party was trying to steer a middle course between the extreme left and the extreme right; it was trying to appear respectable and to present policies which did not openly serve the interests of the working class as against those of the ruling class; it preferred to be seen as a 'national' party instead of a 'working-class' party and to put forward policies which were of 'national' instead of 'class' character. It was, in other words, for greater economic and social justice but it did not threaten the position of the ruling classes especially since it renounced the use of non-parliamentarian means in achieving its objectives. In fact the implementation of its reformist policy measures were the safest guarantee against any violent class struggles or general upheaval in society.

The General Strike of 1926 was important because of its political implications. It represented a direct and serious challenge to the capitalist system and it sought to change it through non-parliamentarian methods. It was these political implications of the Strike that placed the Labour Party leaders in an uncomfortable dilemma. On one hand they did not approve of violence in the pursuit of political ends but on the other they did not want to see the strikers defeated and humiliated. The Conservative government did not suffer from such guilty and ambivalent feelings. It saw the Strike as a threat to the *status quo*, it presented it to the public as a threat to the national interests and it used all the powers of a government, including the police and the Army, to defeat it. The collapse of the Strike meant not only misery to the strikers but 'as important is the fact that the surrender immeasurably advanced the transformation of the workers' movement into a tame, disciplined trade union and electoral interest'.[37]

The collapse of the General Strike, the downfall of the Labour government and the economic crisis with mass unemployment in the 1930s, re-opened the issue whether parliamentary means could ever hope to bring about changes in the capitalist system that were a real threat to the economic position of the ruling class. The official leadership of the Labour Party remained convinced that only parliamentary methods could be used in a democracy and that such methods can be effective. This meant that until the Labour Party were returned to power, little could be done. An increasing number of people in the Labour Party, however, were expressing doubts about the ability even of a Labour government to implement measures which really threatened the ruling class. Tawney cynically remarked that:[38]

> The Plutocracy consists of forcible, astute, self-confident and, when hard-pressed, unscrupulous people, who know pretty well which side their bread is buttered, and intend that the supply of butter shall not run short. If their position is seriously threatened, they will use every piece on the board, political and economic—the House of Lords, the Crown, the press, financial crises, allegations of disaffection in the army, international complications—in the honest belief that they are saving civilization. They will probably yield, though only after two elections, to an overwhelming demonstration of opinion, in which the public shows its teeth; but, as far as major issues are concerned, they will yield to nothing else.

Similarly Stafford Cripps[39] (who was later to become Chancellor of the Exchequer in the Labour government, 1945–50) warned that 'the ruling class will go to almost any length to defeat Parliamentary action if the issue is the direct issue as to the continuance of their financial and political control'. Generally it was being recognized that the parliamentary road to socialism was, if not impossible, certainly harder than the first idealists of the Labour Movement imagined. A Labour government bent on fundamental reform has to face the entrenched position of the ruling class in the industrial field, in the civil service, the judiciary, the mass media and most important in the social values of the country. In these ways the ruling class influences the character of legislation of even the most radical Labour governments. In spite of this realization the Labour Party remained on the whole committed to peaceful means accepting Tawney's advice that 'in the absence of an attempt to overthrow democracy, all nods, hints, winks and other innuendoes to the effect that violence is a card which socialists keep up their sleeves, to be played when they think fit, are ruled out for good and all'.[40] Apart from the moral undesirability of using violence as a means to achieve desirable ends, there was the firm belief that the British public would not condone violence and the fear that the ruling class would react equally violently.

The Second World War was much more fertile in social policy planning than the First World War. There is no doubt that the promised improvements in social services were seen by the government as part of the strategy of winning the war; it was felt that such improvements, in the words of Galbraith referring to the American situation, 'would reassure those who were fighting as to their eventual utility as civilians'.[41] Plans for the re-organization of the education, the employment, the social security and other services were prepared and widely discussed during the war years. The plans for social security appeared in the Beveridge Report published in 1942.[42] It was inspired by traditional thinking but it was expressed in fighting language and thus received national and international acclaim at the time and for many years afterwards. Both political parties accepted it and though it was implemented by the Labour government of 1945–50, the Conservative opposition found little to oppose in principle.

The Report was based on six principles. First the principle of universality, i.e. that every adult in the country should be compulsorily insured against the main risks of income interruption, i.e. sickness, unemployment, disability, old age, death and maternity. This was the logical conclusion of the process started in 1911 and gradually extended to cover most of the working-class population. The Report extended insurance coverage to the middle and upper classes and to those few of the working class not previously covered. Second, the principle of insurance that all these benefits should be paid out of funds collected through contributions made by the employees, the employers and the State. The only criterion for the payment of a benefit is whether the person involved paid the necessary number of insurance contributions. Third, the principle of flat rate contributions and flat rate benefits, i.e. that people with different earnings should pay the same amount in contributions and receive the same amount in benefits. The Report recognized that this system of finance was regressive but it accepted it because the public had got used to it since its introduction in 1911. It recognized that a system of flat rate benefits financed out of taxation or even earnings-related contributions would distribute the financial burden more equitably but the Report felt that such a scheme would be seen as unfair by the general public. Even if this were true, and there was no hard evidence for it, the Report preferred to be led by public opinion than try to lead it. Fourth, the principle of subsistence, i.e. that the amount of benefit should be adequate for physical subsistence only. People who wanted benefits for more than bare subsistence should make their own private arrangements with insurance societies. The level of benefits which the Report recommended was so low, though a slight improvement over existing benefits, that people who could afford it would look for real security to private insurance schemes. Fifth, the principle of national minimum, i.e. that every person in need should receive a benefit for subsistence preferably through the insurance benefits and for those who did not qualify for insurance benefits, through the means-tested assistance benefits. The system of national assistance was seen as a safety net to protect those in need who for one reason or another, did not qualify for insurance benefits or who found their insurance benefits inadequate. It was hoped that only a few would fall through the insurance net in the beginning and that eventually there would be no need for the safety net of assistance. As we shall see later, this was a pious hope that never materialized afterwards. Sixth, administrative uniformity, i.e. that the administration of the scheme should be placed in the hands of a new Ministry with regional and local offices covering the whole country to replace the various insurance societies which had so far administered the insurance schemes. The insurance societies which stood to lose through this change were reassured that there was more than enough work left for them in arranging private insurance schemes for the better-paid since the state insurance benefits were designed for physical subsistence only.

Clearly most of these principles were first established in 1911 and the others were the logical outcome of processes started in 1911. Nevertheless, the Report, as a package deal, represented a significant advance in social policy thinking. It is an excellent example of comprehensive instead of piecemeal planning. There was nothing in it to cheer the heart of any radical or to depress the spirits of any intelligent conservative. It was a middle-of-the-road document and like all such documents it represented no real threat to the position of the ruling class. It carried the political art of building bridges between the social classes started in 1911 to near perfection.

The election of the Labour Party to power in 1945 and the defeat of the Conservatives even though led by the war-time Prime Minister, Sir Winston Churchill, showed that the country was ready for radical social policies. The sacrifices and hardships of the war were endured with the hope that when peace came there would be a more just society for everyone. Since both political parties committed themselves during the war for changes in the economic and social services it can be said that the welfare state is the product of industrialization, that it represents a phase in the development of the capitalist system but it was greatly facilitated by the war. Nevertheless the Labour Party's proposals were more comprehensive and enthusiastic of the idea of a welfare state than those of the Conservative Party, and they won it the General Election in 1945.

The social policy legislation of 1945–50 created a network of comprehensive social services based on varying degrees of compromise between the principle that people have a right to use their wealth to advance the well-being of themselves and their children and the principle that the state has a duty to help every citizen achieve a vaguely defined minimum standard of well-being. Thus the reform in education—introduced by the Conservative-led coalition government—provided better educational opportunities for all but it did not abolish private schools. The reforms in health were the most comprehensive but they still made provision for private medical treatment. The housing and the social security reforms were the weakest for they allowed far too much scope for privately financed services. In the field of social security, insurance societies were excluded from the administration of insurance schemes but in spite of earlier Labour pronouncements they were otherwise left undisturbed, a fact which one commentator has described as 'perhaps one of the largest single reasons why the classless welfare state failed to materialize'.[43] Bearing in mind that the level of state social security benefits was adequate for bare subsistence only, private insurance societies were left with abundant scope to provide services to those who could afford it. A truly socialist policy would have meant the nationalization of all insurance societies, a measure which would have had serious implications for industry, commerce and the general network of finance institutions.

To summarize then the situation on social security: the Conservative-led war-time coalition government set up in 1944 the new Ministry that was designed to take charge of the system of social security and in 1945 introduced the system of family allowances. The Labour government introduced in 1946 the new scheme for insurance benefits for sickness, disability, unemployment, old age, widowhood, maternity and the death grant. In 1948, the Labour government completed the process started in 1934 by the Conservatives and abolished all the remnants of the local authority assistance scheme. Instead the new National Assistance Board with regional and local offices was made responsible for providing means-tested assistance benefits to those who somehow fell through the net of insurance benefits.

Two more observations are worthy of note about the Labour government's post-war legislation. First, the ruling class vested interests in industry, the civil service and the mass media played a very important part in modifying the legislation of this period particularly the legislation on nationalization which was a more direct and serious attack on vested private economic interests. Second, the two-party general agreement on the desirability of the welfare state was the strongest indication that the two parties were shifting their respective positions to a middle course, towards consensus politics. There was more disagreement between the left and the right wings of the Labour Party on the welfare state than between the official leadership of the Labour and Conservative parties. The radical Labour party activist, Miliband observes,[44] 'saw the Welfare State and the nationalization measures of 1945–48 as the beginning of the social revolution to which he believed the Labour Party was dedicated; while his leaders took these achievement to *be* the social revolution'.

The post-war period

Three general important factors have influenced the development of social security in the 1950s and 1960s: the economic prosperity of the country, new views on the concept of poverty and the growing trend towards consensus politics. We shall look at these factors first before examining the changes which took place in the field of social security.

The economic prosperity of the country resulted in a very substantial reduction of unemployment. It averaged less than 2 per cent during the 1950s and almost all through the 1960s. From the workers' point of view it meant not only regular wages but also substantially improved wages. From the employers' point of view it meant increased profits and in view of the scarcity of labour a drive to recruit and to retain labour. Occupational fringe benefits for old age, widowhood and sickness were provided by employers as inducements for their employees. The number of male employees in the private sector covered by occupational retirement pension schemes thus increased from 4·33 million in 1956 to 8·1 million at the end of 1967. If one takes into account the employees in the public sector then the numbers increased from 8 million to 12 million or in proportional terms from nearly one-half of the employed men in 1956 to two-thirds in 1967.[45] A similar trend took place in the case of sickness and widows' benefits. In addition to the occupational benefits, an increasing number of people could afford to make their own private provisions for old age, death or sickness through the increasing field of insurance societies. Both the occupational and the private insurance benefits were deliberately encouraged by both Labour and Conservative government tax policies. The overall result of these trends was the creation of three nations, so to speak, in the field of social security. Those people who were covered by all three types of schemes—the state scheme, occupational fringe benefits and private insurance schemes; those who enjoyed the protection of the state scheme and one of the other two schemes; and finally those who had to rely exclusively on the state social security scheme. This division of benefits is part of what Titmuss called the 'social division of welfare' into three categories, 'social welfare, fiscal welfare, and occupational welfare', which 'are simultaneously enlarging and consolidating the area of social inequality'.[46]

A strong social class bias in favour of the middle classes operates in this threefold social security coverage. In the first place middle-class employees are more likely to be covered by occupational schemes and in the second place they receive benefits that are higher in amount than those paid to working-class employees. Middle-class employees have traditionally been considered as part of the management and have therefore been offered conditions of employment that are more generous than those offered to manual workers. Since occupational benefits are usually related to the employee's salary or wages they benefit more the higher paid employees who, on the whole, are of middle-class status. The whole structure of occupational fringe benefits is an extension of the salary and wage structure and therefore its underlying philosophy has no egalitarian elements in it. In addition, occupational schemes have had a very marked effect on the statutory social security schemes because they have stifled to some extent demands for improvements in the statutory field and because they have helped to strengthen the belief that the state scheme must provide benefits for a minimum standard of living only.

The new views on the concept of poverty, which formed the second factor that influenced the development of social security during the post-war period, were to a large extent the product of the apparent economic affluence of the 1950s. Starting with Booth's study of poverty in London in the 1880s and Rowntree's study of poverty in York in 1899, poverty came to be considered largely as a condition that could be measured and which did not change much over time. Poverty was seen in physiological, physical terms. A person was in poverty if his earnings were not sufficient to obtain the minimum necessary goods for the maintenance of merely physical efficiency. It was a standard just above starvation level since it simply ensured that a person's health was not impaired but provided little above that level. As we shall see in the next chapter this was a questionable measure from the start but it was accepted by the Beveridge Report and formed the basis of the level of social security benefits. The economic prosperity of the 1950s meant that people were less willing to be satisfied with social security benefits of subsistence level. Poverty came to be increasingly seen as a relative concept rather than in static, physical terms. This relative concept of poverty had two meanings each of which had different effects on social security.

The first meaning of the relative concept of poverty is that poverty is more than just the minimum income needed to keep a person alive. It must take into account the living standards of the community. It must reflect, in other words, the increased economic prosperity of the country. Thus the level of social security benefits must be related to the wage and salary standards and they must increase in the same way that wages and salaries rise. The first meaning of the concept of relative poverty then compares the individual poor with the rest of the community and demands social security benefits that provide a standard of living that is acceptable to society. It has an egalitarian strand in it for it aims at ensuring, even if vaguely, that the standard of living of people receiving social security benefits does not fall behind that of the rest of the community comparatively speaking. The second meaning of the concept of relative poverty compares the individual's standard of living when he is at work and when he is out of work. It argues that people at work get accustomed to a certain standard of living and that when they are out of work they should enjoy a comparable standard of living. In other words, the amount of money that people out of work need to maintain themselves must be related to their previous earnings from work. This was, as mentioned above, the basic characteristic of occupational benefits and what was being demanded in the late 1950s was the extension of this principle to the statutory field of social security. We shall discuss later how and when this demand was met but it is worth noting here that this concept of poverty is antithetical to the first for it stresses inequality of incomes among social security beneficiaries. Generally then the relative concept of poverty maintained that 'the meaning of poverty varied not only in relation to the changing standards of the whole society but also in relation to the standards of different individuals within society at a given moment in time'.[47] Social security reflects two fundamental social values in industrial society—that physical poverty is undesirable and should be abolished while income inequality is necessary and should be maintained. In the words of Rimlinger,[48] 'In the mature industrial society, social security . . . has the dual task of eliminating unacceptable manifestations of economic and social inequality and of maintaining inequalities that are legitimate and purposeful.' Whether social inequality is necessary or desirable depends obviously on the individual's viewpoint of society. It is a fundamental value judgement to which we shall return in chapter 3.

The third major factor has affected the development of not only social security but of the other social services as well. This is the political consensus not only among political parties but among intellectuals and the general public. It is a phenomenon common to affluent industrial societies and its causes lie deep in the social, political and economic structure of these societies. The working class is satisfied with the capitalist system and it has lost most of its drive to change the system substantially through peaceful or violent means. It has enjoyed its newly gained relative affluence and its only desire is to increase it. In this respect it has a vested interest to maintain the capitalist system and to press for a higher material standard of living. The intellectuals have given up the nineteenth-century tendency to produce blueprints for radical transformations of society. They have instead taken to piecemeal social engineering which attempts to make the capitalist machine more efficient and more humane in a gradual way. The political parties are agreed on the desirability of the welfare state and the mixed economy. The major political parties claim to represent 'national' instead of class interests and they reject so-called 'doctrinaire' in favour of pragmatic, flexible approaches to the solution of social problems. In this country this shift towards consensus politics between the Labour and the Conservative Parties has been accelerated by the establishment of the network of social and economic services during and immediately after the Second World War. Since then the Labour Party in its policies and in its election manifestos has, as Butler and Rose commented of the 1959 General Election,[49] 'played down any claim to stand, as a socialist party, for a radically different form of society . . . it asked the voters to say that it could administer the mixed economy welfare state better than the Conservatives'.

This 'end of ideology' has been seen by some as a welcome development because ideological blueprints for change have either come to nothing or they have ended in national catastrophes. Bell[50] claims that the trouble with ideology is that it 'makes it unnecessary for people to confront individual issues on their individual merits. One simply turns to the ideological vending machine, and out comes the prepared formulae. And when these beliefs are suffused with apocalyptic fervor, ideas become weapons, and with dreadful results.' Moreover the end of ideology can mark the beginning of an empirical approach to the achievement of utopia. Unlike the ideological approach to reform, an empirical approach has to satisfy the various groups in society, it has to state more clearly what it wants to achieve, how it is going to achieve it, who is to pay and so on. In brief, 'the ladder to the City of Heaven can no longer be a "faith ladder", but an empirical one'.[51] What Bell does not say is that such an empirical approach will be frustrated by the vested interests of the ruling class if and when it attempts radical changes that really threaten its dominant position in society. It is important to point out the concealed ideology behind this thesis. Far from being value-free, it is basically the ideology of gradual small-scale change that leaves the economic and social system basically unaltered. It is a liberal-conservative doctrine.

Writers on the radical left, obviously deplore the political consensus and the end of ideology. They see in this development the negation or the delay of the proletarian revolution, peaceful or violent, which would defeat the capitalist system and replace it with the socialist society. Modern Marxists attribute this development partly to the deliberate flexibility of the ruling class, partly to the mistakes of working-class parties and partly to the weight of the mixed welfare state economy. Some contemporary Marxists view the present political and ideological consensus with profoundly deep gloom for they see no way out of it. Marcuse's thesis of the one-dimensional man has been the centre of considerable controversy for it tries to explain why the working class and the intellectuals in the West have been trapped by the ideology of the technological society and they have become willing slaves to it. 'A comfortable, smooth, reasonable, democratic unfreedom prevails in advanced industrial civilization, a token of technical process,' he proclaims.[52] This polished performance of advanced industrial societies in satisfying people's physical needs, in creating 'false' needs for them which in turn they satisfy, results in a 'euphoria in unhappiness' which makes people content with the social system even though it represses their individuality in thought and action by a constant subtle and all-effective process of direct and indirect indoctrination. Caught in the vicious circle between the social values and the economic affluence of the technological society, individuals and social classes have no power or will to reject the social system or to fight it. 'The totalitarian tendencies of the one-dimensional society render the traditional ways and means of protest ineffective—perhaps even dangerous because they preserve the illusion of popular sovereignty.'[53] Only the total rejection of the benefits and the social values of the technological society by its protegés and beneficiaries—which constitute the bulk of the population—can result in any radical change. Such a prospect seemed unfeasible for Marcuse's one-dimensional man.

Marxists and other radicals have found much to agree with in Marcuse but many disagree on his gloomy prediction that the contemporary industrial society marks the end of all social change. As Horowitz points out,[54] 'At issue is not the notion that the societies of the West may be *passing through* an equilibrium period of social development, but the notion that they have arrived at an equilibrium which *moves through time*, i.e. which can be regarded as final.' He claims that there is no evidence to substantiate Marcuse's *'unhistorical* conclusion that in "advanced industrial society" mankind has in some sense finally come to the millenial kingdom'.[55] Indeed the present consensus is a temporary affair for it is atypical of capitalist societies. The internal contradictions of capitalism are so many and so irreconcilable that capitalism is a system 'perpetually in crisis' that will inevitably collapse. Miliband also takes the same line. He recognizes that:[56]

the forces of attunement at work in advanced capitalist society, whether they are the result of deliberate striving or of the weight of the system itself, are indeed formidable. But this is not at all the same as saying that their combined impact is finally compelling, that they spell with inexorable finality the death-knoll of socialist challenge, that they herald the arrival of 'one-dimensional' man. They constitute one major factor in the equation of class conflict. But the hopes of some and the lament of others that they are powerful enough, together with the 'affluent society', to bring it to an end, to ensure the evacuation of the battlefield by the working classes, and to leave only small and easily manageable bands of guerillas on the terrain—all this constitutes a fundamental underestimation of the profoundly destabilising forces at work in capitalist society, and an equally fundamental over-estimation of its capacity to cope with them. The realistic perspective which advanced capitalist societies offer is one not of attunement and stability, but of crisis and challenge.

The influence of these three general factors—growth of occupational fringe benefits, relative concept of poverty and the end of ideology—on social security will become clear in subsequent chapters. Here we can only summarize their effects using the six principles established by the Beveridge Report as our basis for discussion.

Both the Conservative and the Labour Parties, for different reasons, have accepted the inevitability of earnings-related benefits and thus put an end to the notion that social security benefits should be flat rate. The Conservatives are ideologically at ease with earnings-related benefits for such benefits reflect the values of a capitalist wage system. Unequal social security benefits reinforce an unequal wage and salary structure and vice versa. The Labour Party had to perform an ideological somersault to justify earnings-related benefits but it performed this exercise with remarkable agility. In fact it was the first of the two parties to put forward a plan for state earnings-related benefits in 1957. Its main argument for such benefits rested on the concept of relative poverty and on the pragmatic argument that since they were already provided by employers, the state would merely extend to all people what was the privilege of the few. It is in situations such as these that the thesis of the one-dimensional man becomes clear. A radical Labour Party in power could instead have pressed for equality in earnings from work so that earnings-related benefits would not be necessary. Equality in wages would be reflected in equality in social security benefits. Such a radical policy, however, is so contrary to the values of the capitalist system that it is unthinkable as a serious policy for both the Labour Party and the trade unions. In fact as we shall see later both political parties are agreed that it is not equality of incomes that is a desirable goal for state action but inequality of incomes through the principle of equality of opportunity.

The principle of universality, i.e. that everyone should be covered by the state social security services, has also been changed. The growth of occupational retirement pensions, particularly from the mid-1950s onwards, has meant that many people and particularly the middle classes have enjoyed a dual protection against the economic problems of retirement. One could have argued that the logical policy would have been for the government to improve its own retirement pension and to make the provision of occupational retirement pensions either illegal or very difficult. This would have ensured that every retirement pensioner would have received the best retirement pension that the country was willing to provide. Instead both political parties have accepted the existence of this dual provision for retirement which clearly benefits the better-paid sections of the community. The main difference between the parties is that the Conservatives have done everything to encourage the growth of occupational pensions and are proud of their achievement while the Labour Party have rather reluctantly accepted the inevitability of occupational pensions. We shall discuss this in greater detail in chapter 5.

The principle of insurance has become so much part of the national tradition that it is rarely seriously questioned. From the actuarial point of view it has very little meaning because the insurance contributions which one pays are not enough to pay for the benefits which a man and his dependants receive. Nevertheless, it has all the advantages which we discussed earlier that it has enjoyed strong and loyal support from both political parties. The ill-effects of the application of the insurance principle are either ignored or glossed over as unfortunate but inevitable. In the first place people who have not paid the necessary number of insurance contributions are not entitled to any insurance benefit and must apply for a means-tested supplementary benefit. This group of people includes some of the most tragic cases—people who because of ill-health have worked irregularly or not at all; people who though healthy may have been constantly in and out

33

of work through no fault of their own; and so on. In the second place the insurance principle as it is being used in the proposals of the last Labour government and in those of the present Convative government for superannuation schemes makes the payment of retirement pension, and the amount of the pension so totally dependent on the employment and earnings history of the individual that the economic criteria of the market almost wipe out the social criteria of a social service.

The administrative changes that have been made since 1948 illustrate the conflict in values and in policies with regard to a person's entitlement to means-tested benefits. The establishment of the National Assistance Board in 1948 with its regional and local offices was greeted with general jubilation for it was seen as marking the end of the local poor relief system and particularly the shame attached to the receipt of assistance. Evidence in the 1950s and 1960s, however, showed that a large number of people in need who would qualify for assistance benefit did not apply for it because of the public shame attached to means-tested benefits. As a result the Labour government renamed assistance benefits supplementary benefits, renamed the National Assistance Board the Supplementary Benefits Commission and made a few minor administrative changes intended to make the payment of supplementary benefit mainly to the elderly, but not to the unemployed, easier. In general then governments since the war have followed the conflicting policy of attempting on one hand to liberalize the payment of assistance benefits and on the other to emphasize the importance of insurance benefits. The Beveridge Report[57] quite categorically stated that assistance benefit 'must be felt to be something less desirable than insurance benefit' if the payment of contributions would maintain its public esteem. Successive governments have tried not to highlight this but at the same time they have failed to recognize the sociological implications of means tests in an industrial society which worships hard work, economic incentives and economic achievements. As Coser argues,[58]

> The very granting of relief, the very assignment of the
> person to the category of the poor, is forthcoming only at
> the price of a degradation of the person who is so assigned.
> To receive assistance means to be stigmatized and to be
> removed from the ordinary run of men. In order to be
> socially recognized as poor, a person is obliged to make his
> life open to inspection. The protective veil which is

available to other members of society is explicitly denied to
them. . . . When monies are allocated to them, they must
account for their expenses and the donors decide whether
the money is spent 'wisely' or 'foolishly'. That is the poor
are treated in this respect much like children who have to
account to their parents for the wise use of their pocket
money.

In addition people in receipt of supplementary benefit are visited
at their home by officials, a procedure which, though it may serve
some useful purposes, increases the public visibility of people
receiving benefits as poor, as failures. Moreover, as Pinker has
pointed out,[59] the stigma which poor people feel in receiving
welfare benefits:

is compounded by the fact that even those rights in the
market of which they are most conscious are in practice
often denied them. The poor lack the money to claim parity
in the private market. Normatively and relationally they
learn to define themselves as inferior persons, subordinate in
terms of both money and knowledge. Thus many of the
clientele of social services come to the welfare agency already
stigmatized.

The only radical solution is the payment of benefits to people who
are unemployed, old, sick, etc., without any means test and
without any reference to insurance contributions. This will not
only simplify the administrative requirements for entitlement to
benefit but it will also emphasize the social aspects of the social
security service which are more meaningful than the economic
criteria of eligibility involved in the insurance principle. At the
same time it will replace the humiliating personal means test with
objective proof that one belongs to a population group—the aged,
the sick, the unemployed, etc.—that qualifies for financial help
from the state. It may not do away with the stigma inherently
attached to the receipt of welfare benefits in competitive industrial
societies but it may help to reduce it and will at least not reinforce
it.

The policies of both governments since the re-organization of
the social security services after the war have also resulted in a
greater proportion of the population drawing means-tested assistance and supplementary benefit—the total number of persons
receiving such benefit rose from 1,011,000 in 1948 to 2,738,000 in

1970.[60] In a limited sense this is a desirable development because it reflects the greater willingness of people to apply for help as a result of the partial liberalization process and of the government's publicity of supplementary benefit. In a more important sense, however, this is a retrograde development for it reflects the policies of both governments to raise the level of supplementary benefits more frequently than that of insurance benefits in an effort to help those 'in need' only and not to pay higher insurance benefits to all. In this way Beveridge's idea of the means-tested scheme acting as a safety net has been drastically changed. The role of the supplementary benefit scheme today is not a residual one for a declining minority but a permanent one for a substantial and increasing population group.

Social security services involve the giving and withholding of money—the priceless commodity of industrial profit-orientated societies. Our historical discussion has shown that ruling class power and authority sometimes in the face of working-class opposition and sometimes with the active or passive co-operation of the working class ensured that what social security provision had to be made from time to time always took into account the ideologies and interests of the ruling class either openly or in the name of national interests. Social security services have developed into a complex administrative maze which openly reinforces the inequalities of the wage system and helps to accommodate the working class to its inferior position in the social structure. They act as a medium of social cohesion and in this way they play their part in perpetuating the social system. They rarely act as a means of social change because the criteria of the market dominated them from the time the insurance principle was made the central criterion qualifying for benefit.

2

Poverty and the social security system today

We saw in the last chapter how the problem of poverty was variously defined in the past and that it was only at the beginning of this century that poverty was beginning to be recognized as a social problem which had its roots in the social and economic structure of society and which could be solved by social action. Subsequent events, and particularly the economic depression of the 1930s and the comparative economic prosperity of the 1950s, have provided ample evidence of the view that when the economic system of the country provides work opportunities for all, people will work and maintain themselves. Poverty among the working population is not the result of individual laziness or other personal psychological characteristics but of the inability of the economic system to provide employment for all and to pay adequate wages to all.

The causes of poverty

Generally the view that poverty is caused by personal laziness and irresponsibility has been abandoned among social scientists. This, however, does not mean that the opposite view, i.e. that poverty is the result of the economic system of society, has been completely accepted by all. Ideologies do not usually disappear in such short time. They tend to persist in new modified and concealed forms. It is not surprising, therefore, that more subtle forms of association between poverty and the personal characteristics of the poor have been suggested by various social scientists. The general implication of these views is that in full-employment societies there are enough social and economic opportunities to lift out of poverty all those who have the ability and the willingness to pursue work with some determination. Those who remain poor are, on the whole, those who suffer from a number of personal inadequacies. These personal inadequacies are not all related to character or personality structure; most are the result of the individual's lack of objective potentialities, i.e. education, skill, training and the like. Galbraith's explanation of poverty is representative of this school of thought. He maintains that mass poverty has been abolished in industrial societies and divides what poverty exists today into 'case poverty' and 'insular poverty'. Case poverty is attributable to the personal characteristics of the poor. It is the result of 'some quality peculiar to the individual or family involved—mental deficiency, bad health, inability to adapt to the discipline of modern economic life, excessive procreation, alcohol, insufficient education or perhaps a combination of several of these handicaps'.[1] Insular poverty is due to large-scale unemployment in specific regions of an industrial country. Though Galbraith admits that in the case of insular poverty 'it is not so easy to explain matters by individual inadequacy'[2] he goes on to attribute this kind of poverty as well to the individual. He argues that there is a natural inclination on the part of many people to 'spend their lives at or near the place of their birth. This homing instinct causes them to bar the solution, always open as an individual remedy in a country without barriers to emigration, to escape the island of poverty in which they were born.[3] So whether by instinct, by inborn ability or by their way of life, the poor are responsible for their poverty.

While these explanations of poverty are put forward in understanding sympathetic language, their implication is that the poor are generally unintelligent, handicapped and unimaginative while the wealthy are, on the whole, intelligent, talented and possessed with ambition, drive and industriousness. These views overlook two relevant points. First, many people enter occupations when they are young not out of personal choice but out of accident or necessity. Thus people can find themselves in low-wage industries, in declining industries and they can thus be poor irrespective of of their personal qualities. Second, and more important, these views are based on the ideology of industrialism that unskilled jobs should not be as well paid as other jobs. To put this in a different way, the fact that people who do unskilled work are usually badly paid and many are poor is not due to their personalities or their education or training but to the ideology of the economic system which places a lower value in terms of cash and prestige on the unskilled rather than the other jobs. This emphasis by social scientists and politicians on the educational and other processes through which some people achieve economic success has dominated politics to such an extent that it has left no room for discussion about the legitimacy of the distribution of income and wealth.

An equally damaging view of poverty is the recent much publicized notion of the culture of poverty. According to the main exponent of the culture of poverty thesis, Oscar Lewis, the poor have 'a way of life, remarkably stable and persistent, passed down from generation to generation along family lines. The culture of poverty has its own modalities and distinctive social and psychological consequences for its members. It is a dynamic factor which affects participation in the larger national culture and which becomes a subculture of its own.'[4] The poor have a way of life which is different from that of the general society; it is a way of life generated and maintained by a complex system of social values and as such it is passed on from generation to generation through the process of child socialization. The poor in other words have their social values to blame for the fact that they do not enjoy their due share of the economic prosperity, the educational advancement, the social life and so on of the wider society. The corollary is that in order to remove poverty one has to change the life styles of the poor. Giving them more money, providing better employment opportunities, better educational facilities, will not do away with the culture of poverty which is at the root of their inferior position in society. This view of poverty confuses norms with aspirations. Poor people may well behave differently from the rest of society in certain aspects of their life because of the economic and social situation they find themselves in. It is also natural that they may create values, explanations and justifications for their behaviour. This does not mean, however, that they do not share the aspirations of the wider society. Their behaviour is a realistic response to the situation they find themselves in. It is also ahistorical to assert that the culture of the poor was shaped in the first place by economic, political and social factors over a period of time but that this same culture is not amenable to change by similar factors. It may well be that certain aspects of a culture change less quickly than others when subjected to the influence of a new set of socio-economic factors but basically, as Gans points out,[5] 'culture is a response to economic and other conditions; it is itself situational in origin and changes as situations change'. The notion of the culture of poverty not only disregards or grossly underestimates the part which the existing social and economic system plays in creating social values and in perpetuating poverty but it also has undesirable implications for social policy. As Marsden has commented,[6] the culture of poverty thesis 'implies that we do not need to change ourselves. Instead programmes must

D   39

be directed at fitting the poor to society, at motivation rather than the reduction of discrimination and the provision of genuine opportunity.'

The meaning of poverty

Apart from the causation of poverty what has also changed during this century is the meaning of the concept of poverty. Poverty as first defined by Booth and Rowntree at the turn of the last century meant subsistence living. In the 1950s and 1960s not only was the notion of subsistence living severely criticized in favour of the thesis of relative poverty but two more meanings have been given to the concept of poverty—inequality and powerlessness. Subsistence poverty refers to the lack of the basic necessities to maintain physical health and working capacity. Food, clothing, housing, heating and a group of miscellaneous items are the basic necessities that have to be provided for the abolition of subsistence poverty. As we shall see later in the chapter this definition of poverty was found too rigid by even Rowntree who was its principal designer. Gradually it came to be accepted that poverty is not a static absolute state of affairs but it is rather a changing concept relative to the conditions of society in which it exists. Indeed this was not a new idea for many economists before Rowntree had defined poverty in relative terms. Adam Smith[7] recognized that 'by necessities I understand not only the commodities which are indispensably necessary for the support of life, but whatever the custom of the country renders it indecent for creditable people, even of the lowest order, to be without'. We refer to Townsend's definition later in the chapter and it will suffice here to quote an American opinion on the subject—President Johnson. In his message to Congress on poverty on 3 March 1964, he stated that for the poor poverty 'means a daily struggle to secure the necessities for even a meager existence. It means that the abundance, the comforts, the opportunities they see all around them are beyond their grasp.'[8] In many ways relative poverty is similar to the concept of inequality though it does not involve the whole economic structure of society. It is quite possible for a society to include income inequality without necessarily involving poverty even in the relative sense.

Inequality refers to the stratification system of society. So long as the wealth of the country is unequally distributed there will be poverty in the sense of inequality. To abolish poverty in this sense is to abolish the economic inequalities in society. It is to make the distribution of wealth and income completely equal. To understand poverty one must study wealth for it is the disparity between the two that is the problem. As Rein put it,[9] 'To understand the poor we must then study the affluent.' Poverty as lack of power is a wider concept than inequality. Lack of power in an unequal society entails an inferior status in society and an inability to protect oneself against the discriminating effects of the social, political, economic and legal system of society. This lack of effective resistance against discrimination results in a perpetuation of the vicious circle between lack of power and low status. 'Loss of power,' write Coates and Silburn,[10] 'is the most serious of all losses entailed in poverty, because it is the most permanent and self-reinforcing.' The disadvantages of the lack of power of the poor is better illustrated by looking at the advantages of the possession of property and wealth by the rich. Meade writes:[11]

A man with much property has great bargaining strength
and a great sense of security, independence and freedom;
and he enjoys these things not only *vis-à-vis* his propertyless
fellow citizens but also *vis-à-vis* the public authorities. . . .
An unequal distribution of property means an unequal
distribution of power, even if it is prevented from causing
too unequal a distribution of income.

Lack of power will still persist, though in a modified and reduced form, even when income inequalities are abolished. A society where complete income equality prevails will still provide positions of authority and responsibility. The occupants of such positions, though not receiving higher wages, will still enjoy higher status because of the command they will exercise over other people. This may be a more rational distribution of power and it may be of a less pronounced nature than the power existing in unequal societies but it is power inequality all the same.

The measurement of poverty

Social security is concerned with subsistence poverty and it is this we shall be discussing in the rest of this chapter. In the following chapter we shall look at the question of income inequality as part of the discussion on low pay. The question of poverty in the sense of unequal distribution of power is well beyond the scope of this book for it entails a study of the social system in all its aspects. Industrial societies possess the wealth to abolish subsistence poverty without affecting the position of the ruling class. In fact the threat to the ruling class in an industrial society comes from the existence of large-scale subsistence poverty rather than from its abolition. Unless governments are seen to be making an effort to deal with the problem of subsistence poverty, they will be inviting social unrest from the working class and its middle-class liberal sympathizers. Abolition of subsistence poverty then promotes social stability and thus strengthens the position of the ruling class.

Though the poor as a group are roughly identifiable in society, the concept of subsistence poverty can not be defined precisely and objectively. The cut-off point that separates the poor from the non-poor is vaguely drawn, it is a changing line of division and above all it is subjectively decided by those in authority when it comes to social policy measures. There is no objective neutral definition of poverty. The philosophy behind subsistence poverty and the social security measures designed to deal with it are largely determined by social values which explicitly or implicitly support the existing social and economic system. This will become clear from our discussion on the measurement of subsistence poverty and the level of flat rate insurance benefits which are supposed to abolish such poverty.

The measurement of subsistence poverty and the level of insurance benefits in this country have been greatly influenced by Rowntree's poverty surveys in York in 1899 and 1936.[12] Rowntree was anxious to establish a rigorous definition of subsistence poverty and in doing this he had to find answers to three inter-related questions: First, what is the cut-off point between the poor and the non-poor? Or, in other words, what criterion should be used to decide whether a person was in poverty? Second, what basic necessities must be satisfied before one can say that a person is not in poverty according to the criterion established in the first place? Third, what kind of evidence was to be used to establish whether the various basic needs were met in relation to the criterion of subsistence poverty?

Let us take the third point first because it was the easiest. He used as evidence the opinions of experts, especially nutritionists, the evidence which he collected himself on the way working-class respondents spent their earnings, and the evidence from the opinions of working-class people on what they considered as necessities. In other words, his evidence was partly expert opinion and partly lay opinion reflecting the way people lived as distinct from the way they should live. The two are not completely different because what the experts say people need, what quantities and what quality, takes into account the prevailing living standards. Indeed for some basic necessities, such as clothing, there can be no expert scientific opinion that is divorced from existing living standards. A nutritionist may be able to express an opinion of how much food the body roughly needs to maintain physical health but how can a clothing expert say how much clothing is needed for a person to maintain his health?

Going back to his first question, he used as his criterion of subsistence poverty 'the maintenance of merely physical health.'[13] People whose incomes were not adequate to provide the basic necessities for the maintenance of physical health were in 'primary poverty'. His basic necessities were food, housing, clothing and household sundries which was mainly expenditure on fuel. Nothing was allowed for any other expenditure. This is how he described his poverty line:[14]

A family living upon the scale allowed for in this estimate must never spend a penny on railway fares or omnibus. They must never go into the country unless they walk. They must never purchase a halfpenny newspaper or spend a penny to buy a ticket for a popular concert. They must write no letters to absent children, for they cannot afford to pay the postage. They must never contribute anything to their Church or Chapel, or give any help to a neighbour which costs them money. . . . The children must have no pocket money for dolls, marbles or sweets. The father must smoke no tobacco, and must drink no beer. . . . Should a child fall ill, it must be attended by the parish doctor; should it die, it must be buried by the parish.

Before discussing the methods he used for calculating the quantity and quality of the items that were necessary for physical health, it may be useful to look at his list of needs for his second study in 1936. His main change in 1936 was to enlarge considerably the group of Sundries and allow for expenditure on such items as newspapers, stamps, writing paper, radio, holidays, beer, tobacco and presents. In other words he made allowances for items which satisfy social and cultural rather than physical needs. A person may be able to maintain his health without reading a newspaper or without smoking but having to do without such items marks him off from the rest of the community in such a way that he suffers socially or emotionally. There is no scientific way of deciding what constitutes a cultural need. It can be argued that a need is cultural if the majority of the population are making use of the item in question but a political decision is still needed as to what constitutes a majority as well as a majority of which section of the population. Clearly cultural needs are subjectively decided by the politicians taking vaguely into account the living standards of the community. Thus they vary from country to country and from one period to another in the same country. The three main physical needs, however, of food, clothing and housing are universally accepted as necessary for survival.

This tidy division between physical and cultural needs may be useful for discussion purposes but it has severe limitations for it wrongly assumes that physical needs have no cultural element in them and vice versa that cultural needs have no physical element in them. It can be safely said, however, that all physical needs have a cultural element in them in the sense that their amount and quality are culturally determined. Clothing is a physical need for without clothing a person's health will suffer in this country. Clothing, however, has a cultural element in it in the sense that the clothes which the poor must wear should have some relationship to the prevailing fashions. The same applies to food for as Orshansky has noted,[15] 'Social conscience and custom dictate that there be not only sufficient quantity but sufficient variety to meet recommended nutritional goals and conform to customary eating patterns. Calories alone will not be enough.' The cultural influence on the determination of physical needs is quite evident in the way Rowntree measured food, clothing and housing in his three studies.

The amount of food necessary to maintain physical efficiency was calculated in terms of calories, i.e. the potential energy of food. Rowntree in his first study used the evidence of the American nutritionist, Atwater, who had estimated the minimum diet from his research among American prisoners. Atwater arrived at the minimum number of calories by looking at the amount of food which was needed by prisoners to prevent them from losing or gaining weight. Rowntree varied the number of calories to take account of the fact that women and children do not need as many calories as men and thereby arrived at the minimum requirements for both sexes and for different age groups. It is worth noting that Atwater's diet standard had been tested with prisoners in Scotland and was found satisfactory. It was a standard higher than the standard adopted by European nutritionists which Rowntree examined and rejected. Nevertheless, his standard, like all others, referred to the dietary needs of people over a short period of time and in this way it was inadequate for people to manage over very long periods.

His next problem was to select diets which would provide the necessary calories for households of different sizes. He found another convenient source—this time the dietary tables prescribed by the Local Government Board for workhouses. As if this type of diet was not spartan enough, he chose only the cheapest rations from the workhouse diets. In this way as he himself admitted, his standard of diet was less generous than that achieved by workhouse able-bodied inmates.[16] His last problem was to decide the cost of this diet standard to ordinary housewives. He could not use the prices paid by workhouses for they bought food in large quantities and therefore paid lower prices than the retail prices. He arrived at this cost by averaging the prices paid for such food items by working-class households. Having finally arrived at the weekly cost of his food standard to be used as the line of his subsistence poverty, he renounced it as impractical. He said:[17]

> It must be remembered that at present the poor do not possess knowledge which would enable them to select a diet that is at once as nutritious and as economical as that which is here adopted as the standard. Moreover, the adoption of such a diet would require considerable changes in established customs, and many prejudices would have to be uprooted.

What he could also have added was that not only the poor but the non-poor would not have the intelligence and knowledge or the strength of character and will to implement such a food plan for long.

He faced even greater difficulties in estimating a clothing standard for there was no expert evidence—and there can be no such evidence—as to what people should wear. He therefore chose to base his clothing standard on the opinions expressed by working-class people to his question:[18]

> What in your opinion is the very lowest sum upon which a man can keep himself in clothing for a year ? The clothing should be adequate to keep the man in health, and should not be so shabby as to injure his chances of obtaining respectable employment. Apart from these two conditions, the clothing to be the most economical obtainable.

Clearly this is an impossible question to answer and one can only but question the validity of the replies. Nevertheless the question shows Rowntree's dilemma: how to estimate the minimum expenditure on clothing to satisfy physical needs completely and cultural needs to some extent.

As far as cost of housing was concerned, he gave up altogether any idea of measuring it. Ideally, he said,[19]

> I should have preferred to take some reliable standard of the accommodation required to maintain families of different sizes in health, and then to take as the minimum expenditure the average cost in York of such accommodation. This course would, however, have assumed that every family could obtain the needful minimum accommodation, which is far from being the case.

Instead he accepted the actual amounts paid for rent by his respondents as the necessary expenditure on rent. In brief, Rowntree relied on the expert opinion of nutritionists for his food standard, lay opinion for his clothing standard, and actual expenditure for his housing standard.

TABLE I   *Rowntree's and Beveridge's estimates of minimum weekly expenditure to maintain a family of husband, wife and three children above the primary poverty line*

Items	Rowntree 1899			Rowntree 1936			Beveridge 1938		
	£	s.	d.	£	s.	d.	£	s.	d.
Food	0	12	9	1	0	6	1	10	9
Rent	0	4	0	0	9	6	0	10	0
Clothing	0	2	3	0	8	0	0	5	6
Fuel and light*	0	1	10	0	4	4			
Household sundries ⎱	0	0	10	0	1	8	⎱ 0	6	9
Personal sundries ⎰				0	9	0	⎰		
Total	1	1	8	2	13	0	2	13	0

* For 1899 light was included in sundries.

Rowntree's method of estimating the quantity and quality of the three basic necessities in 1936 were very similar to those he used in his first study. He used a new food standard set up by an expert committee appointed by the British Medical Association in

1933. The minimum standard of diet approved by this expert committee for physical health was not more generous than the Atwater standard though the two were composed differently. If prices are held constant, the amount of money allocated by Rowntree for his food standard was about the same in his two studies. The same observation applies to his clothing standard even though he arrived at it in a different way in 1936. Instead of asking for people's opinions on how much expenditure was necessary for a minimum clothing standard he examined the actual expenditure of his working-class respondents. He used as his clothing standard the average expenditures of a dozen closest replies. He estimated the necessary expenditure on rent by accepting what each individual respondent paid for rent just as he did in 1899.

On the whole his poverty line of 1936 was 40 per cent higher than that of 1899 after taking into account the rise in prices. As we said earlier this was due almost entirely to his liberalization of the sundries group of cultural needs. Though this may appear a substantially more generous poverty line, it was in fact a very modest improvement if it is compared with the rise in wages. Thus the poverty line of 1899 for a family of five represented 79 per cent of the average earnings of male manual workers while the poverty line of 1936 was only 84 per cent. If his two poverty lines are compared with the rise in the economic prosperity of the whole community—not just the working class—there may well have been no improvement at all.[20]

Rowntree's work clearly influenced the level of insurance benefits recommended by the Beveridge Report. In fact the calculations of these benefits had been made in consultation with a sub-committee which included Rowntree.[21] What is surprising is that the level of benefits recommended by the Beveridge Report was the same as that of Rowntree's poverty line of 1936. Since the Beveridge Report referred to the level of benefits in the living conditions of 1938, it was in fact a lower standard when the rise in prices is taken into account. What is even more surprising is that the insurance and assistance benefits which were introduced in 1948 as a result of the reorganization of the social security services were even lower than those recommended by the Beveridge Report when the rise in the cost of living is taken into account. The cost of living index rose by 73 per cent[22] in the ten-year period between 1938 and 1948 while the level of benefits introduced in 1948 was only 56 per cent higher than the Beveridge figure for

1938. In fact, bearing in mind the rise in wages that had taken place in the period between Rowntree's first study in 1899 and the introduction of insurance and assistance benefits in 1948, Rowntree's primary poverty line was more generous than the level of benefits in 1948. Excluding rent, Rowntree allowed 17s. 8d. for a family of five; in 1948, again excluding rent, a family of five would have received in flat rate benefit including family allowances, £2 17s. 0d. In proportional terms, Rowntree's figure was 64 per cent of the earnings of male manual workers while the figure for 1948 was only 41 per cent.

Our discussions on the determination of poverty lines has shown that there is no objective, scientific definition of even subsistence poverty. Ideologies play a major part in deciding what are physical and cultural needs as well as what quantity and what quality is needed to satisfy these needs. The basic assumption behind these ideological considerations is that the amount of money needed to abolish subsistence poverty must not be much higher than the wages of the lowest paid worker. The living standards of the well-paid are not taken into account when subsistence poverty lines are calculated. Only the standard of living of the working class is considered as if poverty was a problem of the working class only and not of society as a whole. The argument that subsistence poverty lines have been calculated in a scientific, objective, fair way is a myth but a convenient one to the ruling class for it serves its interests well. It gives an impression of scientific respectability instead of class ideology. A subsistence poverty line has implications for social policy for it tends to minimize the size of the problem and therefore to reduce government expenditure. It is simply not possible to discuss the measurement, extent and remedies of the problem of poverty in a non-ideological way. As Roach and Roach have said concerning the study of poverty,[23] 'most sociologists are essentially circumspect ideologues for a more benevolent system of capitalism, but are either reluctant to acknowledge their advocacy of conservative social reformism or are oblivious to such a bias'.

The level of benefits

The assumptions underlying the level of flat rate insurance benefits have not been revised by any government since 1948. What has happened is that benefits have been increased from time to time after general discussion in Parliament, the press and elsewhere. Increases have not been automatic but the result of pressures from various interest groups and they have tended to be used for party political propaganda purposes by both parties. Suggestions made in 1946 and afterwards that benefits should be increased automatically with the rise of the cost of living have been rejected until very recently because it was feared that automatic rises could coincide with financially difficult times for the government and thus affect adversely the economy of the country. Such an argument is morally indefensible because it expects the weakest groups in society to bear the brunt of the country's financial difficulties. Recently, however, both governments have accepted the logic for automatic adjustment of benefits to the price index and the present government's proposals are that such adjustments should take place yearly. Though this is a welcome improvement, it does not go far enough. What is needed now is an automatic adjustment of benefits to the rise in wages and salaries so that people on benefits can gain from the rise in the national prosperity as of right and without the long-drawn-out paternalistic political controversies that accompany improvements in benefits.

Insurance benefits have been increased several times since 1948 and today they are higher than when they were first introduced even after taking into account the rise in prices. While the retail prices index increased by almost two and a half times between 1948 and 1970, insurance benefits increased by almost four times. These are overall comparisons and they give a misleading picture for there have been a number of years since 1948 when benefits lagged behind the retail prices index. It must also be borne in mind that the rise in the retail prices index of basic commodities on which most of the income of the poor is spent has been higher than the rise of the general retail prices index.[24] Moreover, when benefits are compared with the rise in wages the picture is not so bright. Until 1965 benefits lagged behind the rise in wages and it is only in the last six years that they have caught up with wages. Thus in 1948 the level of insurance benefits for a married couple was 31 per cent of the average weekly earnings of male manual workers; it remained behind that figure until 1965 when it was improved to reach 34 per cent but it gradually declined so that by October 1970 it was only 29 per cent. The recent rises have restored their value to their 1965 position. Above all it is essential to stress the point that since the rates of benefits were so inadequate in 1948 we are not justified in concluding that they are adequate today simply because they have been improved. We can only measure the present adequacy of benefits if we devise a standard of living index that is relevant to the conditions of today.

Any attempt to establish a new level for flat rate social security benefits must make use of data from three different sources. First, the evidence and the opinion of experts wherever possible. Examples where expert opinion is useful are diet and heating. A great deal of work has been done on the standards of diets that are necessary for adequate living even though all such work has been subjected to criticism. Similarly, the national standard for house-heating set up by the committee under Sir Parker Morris in 1961 can be useful in deciding how much should be allowed for heating in social security benefits. The fact that Booth, Rowntree and Bowley relied too much on expert opinion of minimum needs does not justify our giving up entirely the help we can get from experts in various fields. Expert opinion is useful so long as its advantages and disadvantages are recognized.

The second source of data is the way people live and spend their incomes, for as mentioned several times so far, poverty is a relative concept. As Townsend has said,[25] 'both "poverty" and "subsistence" are relative concepts and . . . they can be defined in relation to the material and emotional resources available at a particular time to the members either of a particular society or different societies.' The Government Family Expenditure Surveys provide a great deal of information about the expenditure of families of different sizes and incomes and though this information in itself cannot determine the level of benefits it can be useful in guiding policy-makers in their decisions. A political decision is still needed on a formula to decide what family requirements should be provided by social security benefits and all one can say is that it is better that the decision on this formula is taken in the light of facts relating to the life of the community rather than be based on guesswork. Political decisions based on facts can better be criticized and evaluated than decisions based on opinions only.

The third source of data is from the way people receiving benefits manage to live. There are clear dangers in relying on data from this source excessively because people try to live according to their means. There is thus the danger of a circular argument— people receiving supplementary benefit spend a certain amount on certain items, therefore their requirement is the amount spent. Nevertheless, used with some understanding, this approach can show in which areas of their daily life people are deprived because of economic factors.

These three sources of data used jointly can provide a great deal of information that can be useful in reaching a decision as to what is necessary for a modest but adequate standard of living that should be provided to people on social security benefits. Clearly it is not an easy question for the answer provided can have repercussions on the way of life of those not in receipt of social security benefits. The more generous the standard of living provided by social security benefits, the more apparent becomes the problem of low wages; and any attempt to deal generously with the problem of low wages, raises the question of income inequality more sharply.

The relationship between the level of benefits and the cost of living or the standard of living has been complicated since the introduction of graduated retirement pensions in 1959 and short-term earnings-related benefits for sickness, unemployment, widow-hood and industrial disability. We said earlier on that the justification of earnings-related benefits holds only if one accepts the existing inequality in wages as desirable or inevitable. If, however, one argues that inequalities in wages and salaries should be evened out, then the state is not justified in providing benefits which reinforce the wages structure. The state should instead ensure that wages and salaries are equal. Both political parties have accepted the desirability of earnings-related benefits and the issues that separate them are on the level of the benefits and the amount of vertical redistribution of income that should be involved.

If the idea of earnings-related benefits is accepted, the question that immediately arises is whether earnings-related benefits in themselves or in conjuction with flat rate benefits should be of the same amount as that of the earnings they replace. If it is true that people get accustomed to a certain standard of living during the time they are at work and that true income security means that the state should provide them with the same standard when they are not at work, then social security benefits should be the same in amount as the earnings they replace. If benefits are lower than earnings, beneficiaries, particularly those who are long-term, will inevitably have to adjust to a lower standard of living. Yet earnings-related benefits are nowhere near the earnings they replace because other considerations have played a part. In the first place it is feared that if wages and benefits were the same in amount, there would be no incentive for people to go back to work. Yet this argument applies only to a very small group of beneficiaries—mainly the unemployed. It does not apply to the elderly and the severely disabled who are permanently out of work nor even to the sick whose return to work depends on the certification of their general practitioner. The second main reason why benefits are lower than wages is financial. If they were the same, the cost of social security would obviously be higher.[26]

The scheme of graduated retirement pensions introduced by the Conservative government mainly for party political purposes in 1959 will be abolished and a new scheme is to take its place which we shall discuss in chapter 5. The earnings-related benefits for sickness, unemployment, disability, widowhood and maternity introduced by the Labour government in 1966 are to be retained. Employed persons contribute $\frac{1}{2}$ per cent of their earnings between £9–30 per week and their employers contribute the same amount. These contributions entitle them to earnings-related benefits of one-third of that part of their weekly earnings which falls between £9 and £30 per week. These benefits are an excellent example of the influence of work values on social policy. They are paid in addition to flat rate benefits for the first six months after which the unemployed, sick, etc., have to rely on flat rate benefits. Yet the needs of the long-term unemployed, disabled, etc., are obviously greater than the needs of the short-term. It was feared that if earnings-related benefits were paid in addition to flat rate benefits indefinitely, people would have no strong incentive to return to work. This fear that people would avoid work is reflected in another way in the scheme: the total amount of flat rate and earnings-related benefits must not exceed 85 per cent of the person's gross wage. The result of this regulation is that the low-paid workers with more than two children suffer.

The extent of poverty

We can now attempt to examine the extent of poverty in society using as our criterion the poverty lines of Rowntree and the level of flat rate insurance benefits which are designed to provide a minimum standard of living. The first study of poverty after the introduction of the new insurance and assistance benefit schemes in 1948 was Rowntree's third survey of York in 1950.[27] His poverty line for a family of five—husband, wife and three children—was considerably higher—36 per cent higher—than the level of assistance benefits. His main finding was that the proportion of the total population in York who lived in poverty dropped from 18 per cent in 1936 to 1·5 per cent in 1950 and that the major factor for this drop was the welfare legislation, including the food subsidies, of the 1940s. Rowntree's findings helped to increase the feeling of complacency in the country that poverty had been abolished. The fact that living standards in York were not representative of those in the whole country was generally overlooked. Indeed the Ministry of Labour report on family expenditure in 1953,[28] unclear though it was with regard to the question of poverty, suggested that Rowntree's figure was an underestimate of the extent of poverty in the country.

It was the studies of the living conditions of the elderly by Townsend[29] and Cole and Utting,[30] of widows by Marris[31] and articles by social workers on the economic position of their clients, that wakened the country to the fact that poverty among this section of the population was still very prevalent. But the study which really brought poverty back to the forefront of national concern was the study of Abel-Smith and Townsend[32] in 1965 based on the government family expenditure survey. Their poverty line was 140 per cent of the national assistance scales to take account of rent and a few discretionary allowances paid by the National Assistance Board to most people on assistance but not included in the basic national assistance scales. Their main findings were that in 1960, 14·2 per cent of the population in the country as a whole were in poverty, i.e. had incomes below 140 per cent of the national assistance scales; that this proportion had risen in the 1950s from 7·8 per cent in 1953, and that the main cause of poverty was low wages paid to people at work. These findings were substantiated by other studies including the government studies of retirement pensioners in 1965,[33] and of families with two or more children in 1966.[34]

The relative importance of the conditions that cause poverty has changed since Rowntree's first study in York. Low wages and old age have been the two main immediate causes accounting for two-thirds to three-quarters of all the people in poverty. In other words both the wage system which is largely beyond the scope of government action and the social security system which is largely a government responsibility are equally responsible for the existence of poverty in the country.

The causes of poverty we have referred to are, of course, the immediate ones for the fundamental causes lie deep in the ideology and class conflict of industrial capitalist societies. All that the studies of poverty have attempted so far is to take a snapshot picture of society at one time in history and to show who are the

TABLE 2 *Causes of poverty as a proportion of all people in poverty*

	Rowntree* 1899	Rowntree† 1936	Rowntree‡ 1950	Abel-Smith and Townsend§ 1960
	%	%	%	%
Inadequate wages	74·1	42·3	1·0	40·0
Unemployment	2·3	28·6	Nil	7·0
Sickness	} 5·1	4·1	21·3	10·0
Old age		14·7	68·1	33·0
Death of chief wage earner	15·6	7·8	6·4	} 10·0
Miscellaneous	2·8	2·5	3·2	

Sources: * *Poverty: A Study of Town Life*, p. 121.
  † *Poverty and Progress*, p. 39.
  ‡ *Poverty and the Welfare State*, p. 35.
  § Adaptation by Coates, K. and Silburn, R., *Poverty: The Forgotten Englishmen*, p. 35.

poor and who are the non-poor at the time of the study. What is much more needed are longitudinal studies which will show, among other things, how the 'cycle of poverty' operates. Rowntree in his study of 1899 observed that the people he found as poor were only a small section of the people who live in poverty at sometime or other in their life. He wrote:[35]

> The life of a labourer is marked by five alternating periods of want and comparative plenty. During early childhood, unless his father is a skilled worker, he probably will be in poverty; this will last until he, or some of his brothers or sisters, begin to earn money and thus augment their father's wage sufficiently to raise the family above the poverty line. Then follows the period during which he is earning money and living under his parents' roof; for some portion of this period he will be earning more money than is required for lodging, food, and clothes. This is his chance to save money. If he has saved enough to pay for furnishing a cottage, this period of comparative prosperity may continue after marriage until he has two or three children, when poverty will again overtake him. This period of poverty will last perhaps for ten years, i.e., until the first child is fourteen years old and

begins to earn wages; but if there are more than three children it may last longer. While the children are earning, and before they leave the home to marry, the man enjoys another period of prosperity—possibly, however, only to sink back again into poverty when his children have married and left him, and he himself is too old to work, for his income has never permitted his saving enough for him and his wife to live upon for more than a very short time.

Such an approach will show not only what proportion of a generation falls into poverty at some time or other during its life time but also which groups of that population are more vulnerable to poverty and at what costs. It may in fact show that for some populations groups among the working class there is no respite in the cycle of poverty for they never manage to lift themselves out of it. Poverty, in terms of inadequate income for a decent standard of living, is not inevitable in industrial societies. Its existence is nothing short of a national disgrace. As Seligman said of the United States,[36] it 'is difficult to become indignant over poverty in an affluent society: such a response was more appropriate to the 1930's. The proper feeling now,' he concludes, is 'disgust'. Its abolition necessitates no major upheavals in the economic and social systems. Why then does it persist in an affluent industrial society?

It is not because society lacks the economic resources for Britain is today wealthier than at any time in the past. The government spends vast sums on military and other related services and it can afford to give away millions of pounds in tax concessions to the better-paid. Industrial societies possess the wealth to abolish subsistence poverty if they have the will to do so. The United States illustrates this thesis. It is the richest of all industrial countries yet it permits as large a section of its population to live in poverty as this country. Sixty years ago Tawney,[37] discussing the prevalence of social problems—including poverty—concluded that the reason they exist was that 'Those who have the power to remove them have not the will, and those who have the will have not, as yet, the power'. Since then, Tawney's party—the Labour Party—has held office for long periods without achieving much more in this field than Conservative governments. We have already referred to the Labour government's performance in the immediate post-war period. The performance of the Wilson Labour government in the 1960s was certainly worse with regard to social reform than that of the Attlee government in the 1940s. In the words of Townsend,[38] the social reform measures introduced by the Wilson government were no more 'than hot compresses on an ailing body politic'.

In subsequent chapters we shall discuss in detail the reasons why various population groups live in subsistence poverty. Here we need only state the broad reasons. There is first the belief we referred to at the beginning of this chapter that the working poor and certain groups of the non-working have themselves to blame for their poverty. In a competitive, profit-oriented society the successful tend to scorn and despise the unsuccessful; they are inclined to believe that if the poor chose to work harder, to have less children or to spend their wages more carefully, they would lift themselves out of poverty. There is, second, the inability of the poor to fight against the constricting forces that hold them in bondage for, as we said earlier, the poor lack political power. This association between subsistence poverty and lack of political power has meant that any poverty pressure groups that have existed have been formed, staffed and run by middle-class sympathizers. It is only during the last five years or so that a new type of self-help poverty group has sprung up which is run by poor people themselves. Both types of pressure groups, however, can only be of political nuisance to governments for they both lack the resources and in some ways they run counter to the ethos of industrial societies to be really effective. Finally, there is the overwhelming preoccupation of society and its governments with increased productivity as a national goal. As we shall show in the next chapter, this preoccupation with productivity has meant that much less attention has been given to the issue of the distribution of income and wealth. So long as the industrial system produces more and more goods and there is a general air of affluence in the country, the question of subsistence poverty tends to be seen as a 'paradox' and to be dealt with in piecemeal fashion with a tendency for social policy to promise more than it is willing to deliver. While all this is happening 'the poor and needy—the millions of them—drag out their drab and dismal lives'[39] in the midst of great and growing private affluence. Yet the situation is not as hopeless as it first appears with regard to subsistence poverty. There are signs that both political parties are slowly beginning to realize that political promises that remain unfulfilled widen that much more the credibility gap between governments and the public. Pressure groups for the poor and to some extent the mass media, too, make it that much more difficult for government to forget their promises. There are also signs that the poor themselves are less willing to suffer in silence indefinitely. It is thus very likely that within the next few years we shall see more definitive plans for the abolition of subsistence poverty.

3

Low pay and
social security

Low pay, like poverty, is a relative concept in the sense that they both have to be seen in relation to the standards prevailing at a given time in society. It is no comfort to the low-paid workers of today to be told that their earnings are many times higher than the earnings of the low-paid workers at the beginning of the century. What matters to them is how their earnings compare with the earnings of other people today for this is what largely decides their standard of living. In this chapter we examine the extent of low pay, the various aspects of social security designed directly or indirectly to help the low paid and finally we look briefly at the question of equality of incomes in society.

The extent of low pay

We shall define low pay in two ways because each definition serves a different purpose. The first definition considers a person's weekly earning as low if they are less than the amount he could have received in supplementary benefit. This type of definition will give us an idea of the proportion of people in full-time work whose earnings fall below the official level of subsistence poverty. It does not, of course, mean that the families of all such workers live in poverty because their earnings may be supplemented by the earnings of their wife, working children and from other sources. Vice versa it does not follow that all those whose earnings are above the poverty line are not in poverty because they may be paying an unusually high rent, have excessively high fares to work, or they may have higher than normal expenses at home because of a physical handicap to a member of their family and so on. Nevertheless, a comparison between low pay and supplementary benefit is useful because it gives a general picture of the inadequacy of wages for family purposes. Thus the various government surveys of earnings have showed that though the risk of a person's wage being inadequate for family subsistence increases with the size of the family, the problem of low pay and family poverty exists with families which have one or two or three children. The government survey of earnings in 1968, according to Atkinson,[1] showed that 2 per cent of men aged over twenty-one in full-time employment earned net wages which were not adequate to support a family of one child at the official subsistence poverty line; the proportion rose to 3 per cent for families of two children; 5·1 per cent for families of three children and 7·5 per cent for families of four children. To repeat, these are not proportions of families of different sizes living in poverty for in many cases there is more than one wage-earner in the family. To gain an idea of family size and family poverty among wage-earners we have to look at the evidence from the Ministry of Social Security Survey in 1966 which took into account all the incomes of families, not just the father's wage, and thus showed lower proportions of families in poverty than those emerging from an examination of the earnings survey. As Table 3 shows, the larger the size of the

TABLE 3   *Families where the father is in full-time work and whose incomes are below supplementary benefit level*

Size of family (no. of children)	Proportion of families of this size with incomes less than NA level*	Proportion of all families with incomes less than NA level which were of this size
	%	%
2	1·3	32·6
3	2·2	24·4
4	3·9	17·1
5	7·4	10·7
6 or more	14·2	15·2
Total	2·4	100·0

* NA allowance includes allowance for rent.

Source: Ministry of Social Security, *Circumstances of Families,* HMSO, 1966, Tables 3, p. 21 and A.4, p. 138.

family the greater the risk that it will be in poverty when the father and sometimes the mother are at work. This does not mean that family poverty among wage-earners is a problem of large families only because the second column of Table 3 shows that almost a third of all such families in poverty included only two children. Both Atkinson's and the Ministry of Social Security Survey figures underestimate the extent of poverty among low-paid workers because they use as their poverty line the supplementary benefit allowance plus rent. This is well below the poverty line used by Abel-Smith and Townsend which is a nearer approximation to the overall level of the supplementary benefit.

The second approach to low pay is to regard as low-paid workers those whose weekly earnings from full-time work fall within the bottom decile of the earnings league. It can be argued that such a definition is meaningless since, so long as earnings are unequal, there will always be a bottom tenth to any earnings league. On the other hand such an approach is useful because one can attempt to find out how the bottom tenth compares with the other sections or with the median of the earnings league and what changes have taken place over the years. It is also useful because 'it recognizes that low pay is essentially a relative problem and helps explicitly to focus attention on that tenth of the workforce which earns less than any other workers; their position can then be considered to see what if anything it is desirable and practicable to do to secure an improvement'.[2]

Using our second definition of low pay we can get some idea of the relative position of low-paid workers in the wage structure. The Prices and Incomes Board Report on Low Pay[3] examined this question for the period 1886–1970 and reached the conclusion that 'the spread of earnings for male workers has changed remarkably little'. The bottom decile of earnings of manual male workers ranged between 66·5 per cent and 70·6 per cent of the median in spite of the fact that wages rose by twenty times during this period. The position of workers in the highest decile has also remained fairly constant varying between 140 per cent and 157 per cent of the median but any benefits resulting from such slight variations went to workers in deciles other than the bottom decile.

TABLE 4   *Dispersion of the average weekly earnings of full-time male manual workers—lowest and highest decile as percentages of the median wage*

Year	Lowest decile	Median	Highest decile
	%	%	%
1886	68·6	100·0	143·0
1906	66·5	100·0	156·8
1938	67·7	100·0	139·9
1960	70·6	100·0	145·2
1970	67·3	100·0	147·2

Source: *General Problems of Low Pay*, Table 1, Appendix B, p. 157.

Clearly the system of free collective bargaining between trade unions and employers has failed to uplift the position of the low paid. In fact, Wootton[4] went as far as to claim that 'not only are the forces making for conservatism in wage discussions themselves strong: the whole tendency of modern methods of wage determination is also to make them progressively stronger'. It is only during the last decade that governments, employers and trade unions have attempted to ensure that the wages of the low paid do not drag further behind the general rise of wages. They have not attempted to reduce the differentials—for in some ways this would be unjust so long as profits remain uncontrolled—but rather to maintain the balance. What has changed during this century is the number of low-paid workers in different industries though some industries have always been 'low pay' industries.

What are the main characteristics of low-paid workers? Though a number of separate factors connected with low pay can be identified it is important to bear in mind that these factors are inter-related with the result that their total impact on individual low-paid workers can be far greater than each of these factors implies. First, women's earnings are lower than men's. A comparison between the median weekly earnings of men and women in full-time occupations shows that women's wages are half those of men and that this relationship has been constant during this century. The latest government survey of earnings showed that in 1971, 87 per cent of all women manual workers earned less than £20 per week, while 87 per cent of male manual workers earned £20 or more. This disparity between men's and women's earnings was found at all levels of the income scale. As Sheridan has commented,[5] 'Statistical quirks apart this grim disparity is hammered home all the way up and down the pay scale.'

TABLE 5 *Comparison between median weekly earnings of full-time manual men and women*

Year	Median weekly earnings		Women's earnings as per cent of men's
	Men	Women	
	£	£	%
1906	1·33	0·66	50·2
1938	3·40	1·61	47·4
1960	14·17	7·58	53·5
1970	25·60	12·80	50·0

Source: *General Problems of Low Pay*, Table A, p. 11.

Age—both young and old age—is another variable related to low earnings. The government earnings survey of 1970 showed that the proportion of male workers aged twenty-one to twenty-four, manual as well as non-manual, earning less than £20 per week was twice the proportion of all men aged twenty-one to sixty-five in full-time work. At the other end of the age scale, those aged fifty to sixty-four, it is the manual workers only who suffer for unlike many of the non-manual they do not benefit from the practice of annual salary increments. Not only is there a greater proportion of low-paid among workers of this older age group but they also suffer from far higher rates of unemployment. Thus the same government earnings survey showed that 43 per cent of the manual workers aged twenty-one to sixty-five who earned less than £20 per week were in this older age group. Skill is another obvious factor. The same survey found that the proportion of unskilled manual workers earning less than £20 per week was more than double that of the corresponding proportion of all manual workers. Health and disability is another factor, though the evidence on this is rather thin. The Ministry of Social Security Survey in 1966 showed that 4 per cent of all fathers in full-time work felt that their earning capacity was limited by ill-health; of those whose earnings were below the national assistance level, the proportion was 14 per cent. Certain regions in the country have higher proportions of low-paid workers than the national average. These are Scotland, Wales, the South Western and the Northern Region, in fact the same regions which have unemployment rates that are higher than the national average. Finally, certain industries contain relatively high rates of low-paid workers. These are obviously industries which contain a high proportion of women, unskilled workers, contracting industries and some of the public services—agriculture, public administration and distributive trades are the three top industries as regards low pay. Nevertheless, it would be a mistake to assume that low pay is concentrated in a few 'sweated trades'. The greater number of low-paid workers are scattered in industries where the general level of pay is high.

We can get a more concrete idea of how low the earnings of workers in the bottom decile are by comparing them with the levels of supplementary benefit—the official poverty line. Generally a man whose earnings are no higher than the lowest decile is no better off than he would be if receiving supplementary benefit if he has four children; if he has five or more children, he would be entitled to receive more in supplementary benefit than he earns though, as we shall see later, this is prevented from happening through the wage-stop rule.

TABLE 6   *Supplementary benefit allowances expressed as a percentage of the net incomes* of all full-time men manual workers with lowest decile and median weekly earnings—November 1970*

Family circumstances	Lowest decile for male manual workers	Median for male manual workers
	%	%
Family with 4 children	98	69
Family with 2 children	88	61
Family with no children	74	49
Single male householder	48	31

* 'Net' income was after the addition of family allowance, less deductions for housing costs, national insurance contributions, income tax and 64p for travel expenses. All families were assumed to be in local authority dwellings in an authority operating a rent rebate scheme.

Source: General Problems of Low Pay, Table I, p. 19.

In principle, there is general agreement between the political parties and the trade unions that the position of the low paid needs improving. A recent White Paper[6] expressed this general sentiment well when it declared that: 'The challenge which faces us as a socially just society is what steps we can take to improve the lot of the low-paid in an affluent society.' The White Paper went on to explain that since there is no one cause but a multiplicity of causes of low pay, there is no one remedy either. In this the White Paper expressed another view shared by the political parties, the trade unions, the employers and other agencies concerned with the wage structure. Underlying these views on the causes of low pay and the remedies proposed there is the fundamental belief in the necessity of an unequal wage structure. This ideological consensus obviously limits the range of solutions to the problem of low pay and confines any differences that may exist between the policies of the political parties to matters of detail. Three plans have been officially discussed and used so far for the solution of the problem of low pay: a national minimum wage, the family income supplement scheme, and family allowances.

A national minimum wage

The controversy surrounding the merits, dilemmas and problems of a system of a national minimum wage is a good example of the crisis in values of an industrial society where profit is the reigning goal of industrial activity. The Report of the Inter-Departmental Committee[7] on a minimum wage exemplifies this crisis in goals and values. On one hand the Report stressed that a national minimum wage would 'prevent the exploitation of weak, ill-informed or isolated groups or individuals and afford them more comprehensive protection than is available through existing voluntary or statutory bargaining machinery'. It would also 'contribute to the relief of poverty amongst employed people, and in so doing would reduce the problem of the wage stop'.[8] These the Report considered as admirable objectives but it went on not only to stress the problems involved but to exaggerate the financial costs of such a scheme with the result that it has put an end, for the time being at least, to the interest that surrounded this issue. The TUC estimated that the Report's figures should be halved while Hughes[9] has argued that 'they should be scaled down even more heavily'. The Report, of course, was reflecting the values of many but particularly of the business community. The conflict in values is between those of social justice on one hand and economic gain on the other. The fear is that if employers have to pay out larger sums in wages to the low-paid workers, this would make economic activity less profitable and since employers would not stand to see their profits suffer, they would either reduce the size of their labour force or increase the prices of their products which would lead to the same result. Increased unemployment would harm the work people themselves and the nation as a whole. The Report spends some time discussing the possibilities of increased unemployment and comes to the conclusion, which is generally supported by economists, that this is inevitable. The extent of unemployment will vary from industry to industry, according to the situation of the labour market, i.e. whether there is a surplus or a shortage of labour and of course the level of the minimum wage. The implied assumption is that industries and firms have been able to operate on the exploitation of the low paid and that a minimum wage would be a financial liability for them. The arguments of the Report against a minimum wage bear some resemblance to the arguments of nineteenth-century industrialists against legislation to prohibit the employment of women and children in certain industries and to limit their hours of work. The fear then was that the country could not afford such measures for they would lead to bankruptcies that would hurt the work people most in the end.

Finally, the Report revived an old argument against a national minimum wage. When the first attempt to introduce such a scheme was made in 1795, the government rejected it because it would not only fail to meet the varying family needs but it would also squander public money on those who did not need it. If the level of the minimum wage was set high to cater for large families, it would be extravagant for the small family; and if its standard was set low to meet the needs of small families, it would fail to lift large families out of poverty. This is, of course, true but it is a fallacious argument because there is no one scheme within the acceptable range of schemes which at one and the same time ensures that no worker gets paid below a certain amount, that does not allocate extra wages to those not in subsistence poverty and which also lifts all working people in subsistence poverty out of it. The government in 1795 turned down the idea of a minimum wage in favour of the Speenhamland system. The government today acted similarly in favour of the Family Income Supplement Scheme which though not the same as the Speenhamland system has several common features.

The advantage of a national minimum wage is that it helps many families out of poverty and it also provides help to many others just above the poverty line. Above all it reduces the exploitation of people at work. So much of the discussion today treats the poverty line as sacrosanct and it tends to assume that all those above it, even if by the smallest of margins, are not in want of financial help from the government or through the efforts of the government. To achieve anything, however, a minimum wage must be at a level that is above the wage of a certain proportion of male wage-earners. The highest quoted figure, so far, is that the minimum wage should be 70 per cent of the median wage of male manual workers. This figure is the dividing line between the wage of the male manual workers in the lowest decile of the wage league and the wage of the other manual workers. It can therefore be of help to about 10 per cent of the male wage-earners, mostly the young and the old, but it will be of help to a considerable proportion of women workers—about 80 per cent of those in full-time employment.

Reading through the Report one is struck by its unspoken

assumption that nothing must be done to disturb the existing system of income distribution. The Report nowhere considers the possibility of limiting profits to pay for a minimum wage, the imposition of a maximum as well as a minimum standard for wages and salaries or complete equality in incomes. The Report is a revealing document for it shows that though the advisability of reforms is determined by undeclared ideological commitments, it is presented to the public under the smokescreen of factual objectivity.

In many ways the application of a national minimum wage will be an extension of existing practice for there are today sixty Wages Councils enforcing minimum wages in industries employing four million workers or about one-sixth of all employees. These Wages Councils evolved from an Act in 1909 which was designed to protect workers in sweated industries by laying down minimum wages. That these Councils have not achieved much is indicated by the fact that half the low-paid workers today are employed in industries covered by these Councils. Their failure is due partly to the fact that the level of minimum wages has been fixed on the basis of largely economic instead of social justice criteria and partly by the fact that minimum wages have not been upgraded frequently enough. Since the industries covered are the non-expanding industries, minimum wages have tended to be well below the national average. The experience of the Wages Councils illustrates a well-established principle in social administration, i.e. that the chaotic forces of industrialism cannot be controlled by half-hearted state action. The danger in the case of the national minimum wage is not only that it will not be enacted because of resistance from the business community but also that if enacted its application will be undermined so that it will achieve much less than it promises.

The prospects of increased unemployment through the application of a minimum wage are real and cannot be ignored. As Hughes points out,[10] however, they do not constitute an argument against a minimum wage policy but rather for 'suitable accompanying measures' taken by the government to buttress the effects of a minimum wage on employment and price levels. These 'accompanying measures' include tax concessions and price subsidies to specific industries and products adversely affected by the application of a minimum wage. In this way, the minimum wage becomes 'only one element in a complex economic strategy' of the attack against poverty.

Family income supplement

The rejection of a national minimum wage and the adoption of a family income supplement scheme stems from the government's ideological commitment to the relief of subsistence poverty rather than to the promotion of social policies designed to reduce income inequality in society. The government view and of those who support the family income supplement is that only people below the poverty line need help and that any government assistance to those above it is a waste of national resources. We shall return to this theme later but let us first describe what the family income supplement involves.

The family income supplement scheme aims at supplementing the family incomes of low wage-earners.[11] It is paid only to families where the main breadwinner is in full-time employment and where the gross family earnings, i.e. those of the husband and the wife, inclusive of family allowances, fall below a certain amount which varies with the number of children in the family. A family with one dependent child is assumed to need £20 per week gross income regardless of what rent the family is paying or what special expenses it may have or whether there is one parent or two in the family. For each additional child £2 are added to the prescribed weekly amount. The government supplement is half the difference between the family's gross income and the prescribed amount but there is a limit of £5 per week to the supplement that can be paid to any family. The supplement is paid after an application is made and investigated by the Supplementary Benefits Commission.

Undoubtedly the family income supplement represents a departure from traditional government practice of not directly subsidizing wages. Though it is insignificant in terms of the total government expenditure that it involves, it is a significant departure from previous social policy especially in view of the government's intention to use it as the first step towards a wider negative income tax scheme. Following the Speenhamland system it has come to be accepted that direct government subsidy of wages is undesirable for it can have adverse effects on the workers' incentive to work harder or longer and earn more. This argument can only have any force for those workers whose weekly earnings are just below the prescribed amount of the weekly supplement. Those whose earnings are well below or well above the prescribed amount cannot be affected. There is no directly relevant evidence but what indirect evidence there is from the effect of income tax rates on work incentives shows that high tax rates can influence some people to work harder, other people to work less hard and they have no influence on others.[12] Whatever the evidence may suggest the government accepted the belief that supplementation of wages undermines work incentives and this is why the family income supplement amounts to only half the difference between the prescribed amount and the total family income. What in effect the government is saying is that people at work should not be helped to rise even up to the subsistence poverty line for fear of affecting work incentives. But what is the logic of the £5 weekly maximum that can be paid to any family as a supplement? It is as simple as it is unjust—government aid must not be so substantial as to make the whole scheme of family income supplement expensive or to be seen as a bounty for large families.

As if all these limitations to the scheme were not enough, the government added an even greater deterrent by making entitlement to the benefit dependent on individual application instead of using the administrative machinery of the Inland Revenue to find out who is entitled and paying the benefit automatically. Means-tested benefits have shown a very low take-up rate and the family income supplement is no exception. We do not know exactly what the take-up rate is since there are no reliable statistics of low pay but it is estimated by the government that about 45–50 per cent of those entitled to the supplement are receiving it. The total expenditure on the scheme was estimated by the government to be £8 million per year but since the take-up rate is about half of what the government expected, the real expenditure is more in the region of £6 million, or about the cost of an aeroplane.

This gives some indication of the government's view of poverty, its extent, its nature and the policy measures needed to deal with it. The family income supplement is less generous than the Speenhamland system though they both stem from the same ideological beliefs on the nature of inequality and poverty. These are that inequality is inevitable and necessary and it does not fall within the scope of State action. Poverty is seen in subsistence terms and any effort to relieve it must be tempered with the value of individual responsibility and self-reliance. It is better that people should be in subsistence poverty rather than the government taking the imaginary risk of affecting their incentive for harder work. The family income supplement is a blatant social class policy measure designed to reduce government expenditure and openly admitting that allowing people to live in poverty is not unreasonable. The fact that it has helped many families does not justify its existence for there are other ways of achieving the same end.

Family allowance

The third social policy measure which provides financial aid to the low paid is the scheme of family allowances. It is obviously a mistake to consider this as a social policy measure for the low paid because it provides allowances to all families with children irrespective of the parents' income. Moreover, any discussion on family allowances is not meaningful unless it is related to the provision of child tax allowances. We shall first discuss these two schemes separately, look at their combined effect on family income and then discuss suggestions for improvement.

Child tax allowances were introduced in this country in 1909 and their basic function was to help adjust the burden of taxation with the individual's ability to pay. A man with children to support has not, on the whole, the same capacity to pay income tax as another man with the same income but with no dependent children. Child tax allowances exempt a certain amount of the father's income from taxation for each dependent child. Thus the more children there are in a family, the larger the amount of the father's income that is exempted from taxation. The exempted amount increases also with the age of the children because the cost of maintaining a child increases with its age. There is no disagreement about the desirability of using the age and the number of children to determine the amount of a father's income that is treated as tax free. What is strongly contested, however, is that the real financial benefit to the father from the tax-exempted income should be greater for the higher than the lower income groups. This is the inevitable result of the progressive nature of the taxation system. The rates at which income tax is paid rise with higher incomes and therefore the same tax free amount of income produces different benefits to tax payers of different incomes.

Family allowances on the other hand benefit the lower income groups more than the higher income groups. An allowance is paid for every dependent child in the family, except the first, and though the amount of the allowance paid is not related to the father's income, the net benefit of the allowance diminishes with the rise in the father's income because the allowance is taxable. Thus only families with very low incomes enjoy the full value of family allowances. Other families get partial benefit as the father's income increases. There is, however, no allowance for the first child and the amount of the allowance does not increase with age though the allowance is slightly less for the second child than for subsequent children.[13]

The combined value of the child tax allowances and the family allowances is complicated but generally it rises with family income. In other words the existing system of government financial aid to children benefits the higher income groups more than the lower income groups. This is a good enough reason for the reform of the existing system but it is not the only one. The combined value of the two benefits is not enough even for a subsistence standard of living for children. For the family man who pays income tax at the standard rate, the combined value of the two benefits is equivalent to the supplementary benefit allowances for children with the exception of the first child which is much less as there is no family allowance for the first child. For a family man, however, whose income is low the combined value of the two benefits is well below the supplementary benefit level of allowances for children.

Why are benefits for the children of working fathers less than the benefits of children whose fathers are out of work drawing supplementary benefit? The simple answer is that these schemes were not designed to provide benefits of even subsistence level. This, of course, begs the question as to why they were not so designed. The child tax allowances were introduced not to help families in poverty or near poverty but rather to provide tax relief for all fathers at work with children. Their relationship to and effect on poverty is incidental. The family allowances were, however, introduced specifically with the aim of relieving poverty but for clear ideological reasons they fall far short of their promise. The ideological reasons were explicitly given in the Beveridge Report. In the first place the amount of the family allowances was based on estimates of the cost of meeting physical needs only, i.e. food, clothing and housing. No account was taken of the cost of cultural needs such as toys, books, sweets, entertainment, etc., which are just as essential to the physical, emotional and intellecttual development of children. Having determined the amount needed for the minimum physical needs of children, a second ideological argument was used to limit further the amount of the family allowance. This was that the State should not meet the whole cost of minimum physical needs because it could undermine the responsibility of parents towards their children. This is clearly a modified version of the nineteenth-century view of less eligibility however subtly it may be concealed in the colourful language of the Beveridge Report. 'The principle of social policy,' the Report declared,[14] 'should not be to remove all responsibilities from parents, but to help them to understand and to meet their responsibilities.' Thus the Report suggested that the way the state should meet part of the cost of the minimum physical needs of children was not to pay any allowance for the first dependent child in the family. It was felt, though no evidence was provided, that a father's wages were adequate to maintain himself, his wife and one child above subsistence level even if the arrival of the first child often involves a severe drop in family income because the wife gives up work. The Report did not stop there but went on to explain that the government did not have to meet its share of the cost of maintaining children in cash completely but could meet it in part by providing services in kind such as free school meals and free school milk. The Labour government accepted all these recommendations with the result that family allowances were far too low from the start. They have since deteriorated in value because school meals, school milk and food subsidies have been either abolished or reduced considerably. Moreover, until the mid-1960s they were allowed to lag behind the rise in prices and wages and it is only since 1964 that they have been increased to regain the low value which they had when they were first introduced. Thus in 1948 the family allowance for the second child was 3·7 per cent of the average earnings of male manual workers whereas in 1971 it was 2·9 per cent. If one allows for the fact that the allowance for the third and subsequent children is slightly higher today than that of the second, while in 1948 they were the same, one cannot but conclude that family allowances do not contribute proportionately more to the family income today than they did in 1948—in fact the opposite may be true.

Before we can decide whether a certain social policy measure is desirable or not, it is important to state clearly what problem we have in mind that needs solving. Unless the ends are stated clearly, there can be confused discussion about the desirability of the means to achieve these ends. It is also possible that more than one end is considered desirable in which case more than one policy measure is necessary. If the problem in question is the exploitation of the low-paid workers then clearly a minimum wage at the level suggested earlier which is regularly upgraded is the answer. A minimum wage will also have other incidental effects such as the relief of subsistence poverty among some families where the father is at work. It will also narrow the gap between the earnings of the lower paid workers and other workers. These, however, are incidental effects, important and desirable though they are. The direct and primary effect of a minimum wage is the abolition of the extreme exploitation of low-paid workers by employers.

If the problem we have in mind to solve is the existence of subsistence poverty among the families of wage-earners, then an improved version of the family income supplement is the social policy we need. Several of the weaknesses of the family income supplement can be remedied by turning it into a generous negative income tax scheme or even by the idea of tax credits proposed in the recent Green Paper.[15] Payment of supplements can then be based on a person's income records with the Inland Revenue and can be automatic instead of being dependent on personal application and personal investigation. In this way the take-up rate of the supplement can be improved to cover all the families of employed men in poverty and the stigma of having to apply and receive benefit can be reduced. Similarly the amount of the supplement can be increased to cover the whole difference between the family income and the prescribed amount. These are desirable and worthwhile improvements but they leave unaltered the basic ideology on which the whole superstructure of the scheme is built. This is that poverty is of a subsistence nature, that it is possible to separate the poor from the non-poor and that social policy should be concerned with the poor only. Clearly for those who believe that poverty is relative and it is in the final analysis similar to inequality any form of family income supplement is only a palliative. Economic growth by itself does not alter income inequality and those who consider inequality undesirable must look to the State for policies designed to reduce or ideally to abolish it. The recent suggestions that social policy should use a 'poverty band'[16] or a 'zone of uncertainty'[17] instead of a poverty line can lessen the iniquities of selectivity measures but they do not do away with them. The broad idea behind these suggestions is that a 'poverty line' is too sharp a division between the poor and the non-poor and that those whose incomes 'are barely above' the poverty line are also poor and need help from government social policies.

For those who feel that the aim of social policy should be to help all families with children and not just those in subsistence poverty only, the answer lies in an improved family allowances scheme such as that put forward by the Child Poverty Action Group or by Sir John Walley.[18] Both plans envisage the amalgamation of the existing schemes of child tax allowances and family allowances into a new scheme which will provide one allowance for every child in the family, free of tax and at a much higher level so as to meet fully at least the cost of physical needs for children. Such a scheme will not only abolish subsistence poverty among the families of fathers in employment but it will also provide help to families with children living above the poverty line. The rationale of this policy is that the future of society depends on its children and it is therefore sound policy for the State to take full responsibility for their physical maintenance just as it has taken over responsibility for their education. As Bell has pointed out,[19] 'a post-industrial society comes to focus on children, if only for utilitarian reasons, because the whole progress of a large-scale society depends so much on this resource and its use'. State responsibility for the full cost of the maintenance of children will not undermine parental responsibility, as Beveridge feared, but it will strengthen it.

It is quite obvious that such a new family allowance scheme, in spite of its tremendous merit, will not abolish inequality in society and it is therefore considered as a half-measure by those who believe in an egalitarian society. For the supporters of an egalitarian society, the new family allowance scheme makes sense only if the wage of the main wage-earner in each family is equal in amount irrespective of their job or their age. The family allowance will then serve the purpose of ensuring that married people with children are not worse off than single people or married people without children.

Equality and low pay

A full discussion on the question of equality is beyond the scope of this chapter for equality is a much wider issue than social security as dealt with in this book. Nevertheless a brief discussion of the relationship between low pay and equality is justified for as we said in the last chapter and as Clegg reminds us,[20] 'Any policy for dealing with low pay has to concern itself with equal pay.'

In spite of increased economic prosperity, inequality in income and wealth is an obvious and a generally accepted feature of contemporary British society. Wealth and income, though related, are two separate issues and arguments for the abolition of wealth inequalities are not necessarily arguments for the abolition of inequalities of incomes from work. Statistics on the distribution of both wealth and income are neither comprehensive nor completely reliable but the picture that emerges is that inequalities in wealth are greater than inequalities in income and that for both types of inequality any reductions that have taken place during this century have been limited.[21] We shall concentrate our discussion on income inequalities rather than on wealth inequalities partly because it is more relevant to our general theme of low pay and partly because there is more agreement on the abolition of private wealth and its inheritance than on the abolition of income inequalities. Socialist countries have done away with private wealth but they have retained and at times they have encouraged income inequalities. The inheritance of wealth is in some ways contrary to the ethos of capitalism for it runs counter to the basic social value that rewards in a capitalist society must be proportional to individual ability and exertion. Thus one can envisage the abolition of wealth inheritance in both socialist and capitalist countries.

Inequality in incomes is justified as necessary primarily because it is considered to be functional to the economic prosperity of the country. Income inequality is necessary as a societal mechanism for motivating people to work hard in order to occupy positions of authority and responsibility and also for encouraging people in such positions to fulfil their duties to the best of their abilities. In the words of Davis and Moore,[22] 'the main functional necessity explaining the universal presence of stratification is precisely the requirement faced by any society of placing and motivating individuals in the social structure. As a functioning mechanism a society must somehow distribute its members in social positions and induce them to perform the duties of these positions'. Tumin's[23] criticism of the functional thesis of inequality brings out its weaknesses well. He points out that in the first place talent necessary to fill the positions of authority is not necessarily limited because we do not know how much talent exists in a society. A stratified society makes the problem worse because it does not allow all talent to fulfil itself. The existence of inequalities makes the fulfilment of the talents of deprived groups difficult and it also means that the allocation of positions of authority is not always done according to talent. Tumin's second main point is that there are other motives, besides high income, which can motivate trained and able people to occupy the 'top' jobs and to carry out their duties to the best of their abilities. There is an understandable tendency to assume that the traditional methods which society has used for the distribution of wealth and income are 'natural', i.e. they are unalterable for they are the result of biological human drives and instincts. This is clearly a mistaken view. Such methods are 'conventional', to use Rousseau's categorization, i.e. they are man-made and they can be changed. A society can be built on co-operation as well as competition, on equality as well as inequality, on national as well as private organization of industry.

In spite of these and other criticisms of inequality, there seems to be little voiced support for the idea of complete income equality. Many have advocated the abolition of wealth inheritance but few have supported the idea that everyone should receive the same income from work irrespective of his occupation. It is somehow felt that complete income equality is as undesirable as extreme inequality. What is needed is moderate inequality. In the view of an American writer,[24]

> Extreme inequality has one set of disadvantages. Exact
> equality would have another. It is possible to avoid them
> both. Society can escape the unhappy consequences of the
> one extreme without plunging into the obvious difficulties
> of the other. It can eliminate the abuses of inequality
> without abandoning its uses. It need only eradicate the
> extremes and with them the evils which they entail. The
> moderate inequality which will remain can be productive of
> little harm and much good.

This view of the desirability of moderate inequality has its British counterparts. The staunchest modern advocate of equality, Tawney, argued that there should be universal social services and adequate wages to enable everyone to enjoy a satisfactory standard of living but over and above that inequality was justified and necessary. 'No one thinks it,' he wrote,[25] 'inequitable that, when a reasonable provision has been made for all, exceptional responsibilities should be compensated by exceptional rewards, as a recognition of the service performed and an inducement to perform it.' If Tawney is apologetic in his acceptance of moderate inequality, Crosland, writing in the era of the Welfare State, shows no doubts or hesitations. In fact he welcomes it. 'We do not want,' he says,[26] 'complete equality of incomes, since extra responsibility and exceptional talent require and deserve a differential reward.' Since 'responsibility' and 'talent' are vague concepts that will inevitably be interpreted in many different ways, it is difficult to see how they can be uniformly applied in wage determination apart from the ethical argument why these two concepts are singled out. Why not, for example, 'training', 'risk' or 'unpleasantness' of the job, and so on?

The concept of 'moderate inequality' or 'conditional equality' is vague enough to be accommodated within the prevailing social and economic system of inegalitarian societies. What is moderate inequality to one observer can be excessive inequality or excessive equality to others. What are considered good reasons for paying some more than others for their work will be open to discussion. By creating divisions of opinion among the egalitarians the concept of 'moderate inequality' ensures the continuance of the *status quo*. 'Change,' wrote Wootton,[27] 'requires justification: the strength of conservatism is that it is held to justify itself.' In this way complete equality is considered Utopian while conditional equality is too vague to be effective. Thus egalitarians are left without a firm policy. Rees, referring to the principle of equality in general, commented,[28] 'Absolute equality is not seriously held by any liberal or socialist thinker, and the principle of conditional equality has shown itself to be too open-ended to convey the substance of what egalitarians are after.'

A necessary part of the idea of moderate inequality is the notion of equality of opportunity, i.e. meritocratic equality favoured by both major political parties in this country. According to this view, society will still be stratified economically and socially but this inequality will be arrived at through the process of equal opportunity rather than through birth, wealth, nepotism or favouritism. Crosland, one of the Labour Party strong advocates of meritocratic equality, has this to say in discussion:[29]

> The essential thing is that every citizen should have an equal
> chance—that is his basic democratic right; but provided the
> start is fair, let there be the maximum scope for individual
> self-advancement. There would then be nothing improper
> in either a high continuous status ladder . . . or even a
> distinct class stratification . . . since opportunities for
> attaining the highest status or the topmost stratum would be
> genuinely equal.

Apart from the fact that it is impossible for everyone to have an equal chance in education and selection for a job in a stratified society, it is worth pointing out that this notion of equality 'is perfectly compatible with a modern capitalist order. Indeed, its emphasis on the most efficient use of talent would in many ways make a positive contribution to such an order.'[30]

The notion of 'moderate inequality' is useful for strategic purposes only. It is clearly impossible for society to change from a vastly unequal to a completely equal distribution of income in a short period of time. Changes will come about slowly and the notion of 'moderate inequality' will act as the means to the ultimate end of complete equality. Reductions in inequality are not ends in themselves; they become merely the platforms from which demands for further reductions in inequality are made. It is in this gradual and progressive way that complete equality will be achieved. 'Moderate inequality' is the means to an end or a stage along a process but not an end in itself.

The idea of complete equality in economic rewards has not gained much support for a variety of reasons. First it runs counter to other social values—individual freedom and individual achievement—which appear to command wide support in society. Increased industrialization seems to have made possible the acceptance of the view that individual happiness is synonymous with individual economic prosperity and that economic prosperity is dependent on individual competitiveness. Co-operation and equality are marginal values, pretty icing on the cake but dispensable trimmings. Individualism is the official reigning social value and other values are subordinated to it. Whether equality is in fact subordinate to individualism as far as the masses of the people are concerned it is difficult to know for there is no relevant evidence. What matters for government policy, however, are the values of the upper classes for they decide the broad ideological framework within which the smaller everyday battles on social and economic issues take place. The second reason is the increase in general economic prosperity in the community. This has been falsely seen as the result of vertical income redistribution rather than the result of increased industrial production. Whatever reason the public may associate with their higher standard of living, economic prosperity has abolished most of the gross and obvious suffering which was to be found in society before the war. In this way it resulted temporarily in a form of complacency. Yet there are opposing trends in public opinion. The demand for the abolition of poverty is much stronger; the traditional criteria for wage determination are not as readily accepted; the demand for a national minimum wage receives strong trade union support; and above all the comparison of present-day economic conditions with those of pre-war days has less and less meaning as the people who lived through those years die. Third, the notion of equality of opportunity coupled with the evidence that social mobility is possible has made inequality in the eyes of many people less objectionable, less of a social problem. It is true that most social mobility takes place between adjacent social classes and only in rare cases the popular dream of 'rags to riches' becomes a reality. Nevertheless the exceptions are used as evidence that the ideal is within the grasp of everyone who tries hard. Again there are opposing trends. It is increasingly being realized that the much heralded principle of equality of educational opportunity has delivered much less than it promised. There is the demand now for comprehensive education, for 'positive discrimination', for greater opportunities for working-class young people in higher education, and so on. There is also better realization that educational opportunity, housing conditions and economic circumstances are inter-related and that you cannot deal with one effectively unless you also deal with the others.

Whatever the theoretical reasons may be, there is also the more important practical reason that any radical move towards reduction, let alone abolition, of income and wealth inequalities is strongly resisted by the rich and the powerful in society. With a few eccentric exceptions, the rich have always opposed ideas for equality. 'The grounds,' for this rejection, says Galbraith,[31] 'have been many and varied and have been principally noted for the rigorous exclusion of the most important reason, which is the simple unwillingness to give up the enjoyment of what they have.'

So long as individualism and competitiveness remain the dominant values for state action, low pay will continue to be prevalent. The abolition of low pay in advanced industrial societies depends more on radical changes in the dominant values than on economic factors. It is important to recognize the effect of social values on social and economic policies for governments in democratic societies cannot, even if they want to, legislate too far ahead of public opinion on basic issues affecting the livelihood of everyone. We referred earlier to Young's generally accepted view in the eighteenth century that poverty was justified for it performed the socially desirable function of making ordinary people work. This notion has today been largely abandoned but a modified version has been accepted. If we were to paraphrase Young's view with reference to inequality today it would run something like this:

78

'Everyone but an idiot knows that earnings from work should be unequal or no one will ever be industrious'. It is the rejection of this philosophy that is necessary to pave the way towards 'moderate inequality' in the first place and complete income equality in the end.

4

∽∽∽∽∽∽∽∽∽∽∽∽∽∽∽∽∽

Unemployment and
social security

∽∽∽∽∽∽∽∽∽∽∽∽∽∽∽∽∽

We concluded the last chapter by saying that a major challenge to
industrial affluent societies is the need to distribute the national
income among all citizens equally. The provision of employment
to all is another such challenge and a necessary prerequisite to
equality. In this chapter we examine the nature, extent and causes
of unemployment in this country before looking at the provisions
which the social security system makes for the unemployed.
Benefits for the unemployed constitute only a small proportion of
the total expenditure by the social security services—about 3 per
cent—yet they arouse some of the strongest emotional reactions
in the community. On one hand there is the general dislike of
having to rely on unemployment benefit and on the other the
suspicion by some that many of the unemployed who draw benefits
are abusing the system. Contradictory though they may appear,
these attitudes are in fact complementary. They both flow from
society's primary social values of work and self-reliance that are
firmly embedded in the industrial culture of this country.

The unemployed

It was only a few years ago that severe unemployment in this
country was thought to have been eradicated for good. The
national rate of unemployment averaged 1·5 per cent per year
during the period 1948–60 and 1·6 per cent for the years 1960–66.
There were isolated years when the unemployment rate surpassed
slightly these average levels but it soon dropped to lower figures.
Up to 1966 unemployment was a serious problem only in the
so-called development areas of the country but at least there was
the consolation that those who were able and willing to move to
the South East and the Midlands could find employment easily.
Since the end of 1966, unemployment increased slowly but
steadily so that in January 1972 it stood at the highest level since
the war—4·3 per cent. Official unemployment rates underestimate
the size of the problem for they refer only to those unemployed
workers who are registered with the Department of Employment,

mainly because this is a condition to their receipt of unemployment or supplementary benefit. Many of the unemployed—mainly married women and elderly workers above retirement age—do not register with the Department of Employment because they do not qualify for such benefits. In general, official unemployment rates are considered to underestimate the extent of unemployment by about 1 per cent.[1] Before we look at the reasons for this recent rise in unemployment it is worth considering some of the structural characteristics of the unemployed.

There is to begin with a substantial difference between the unemployment rate for men and for women—that for men being about three times the unemployment rate for women. This difference is not due entirely to the under-registration of the women unemployed. There is a real difference between the two rates because on one hand women tend to be employed in the expanding white collar or service industries, while on the other the employees of contracting industries are mainly men. Moreover, as Showler points out,[2] the discrepancy between men's and women's wages is a factor in favour of women's employment. 'At a stage of technological development which is now tending to increase the range of work that can be done by *either* men *or* women, then, other things being equal, employers are going to prefer women workers at lower pay rates to male workers at higher rates.' One can also add that a predominantly female labour force is less likely to press its claims for higher wages vigorously through industrial action as men would.

Age is another important characteristic of the unemployed. The official statistics show that the older workers—above the age of fifty-five—and the younger workers—below twenty-five—are more severely hit by unemployment than the other groups. This similarity between the older and the younger group of workers is deceptive, however. Younger workers are more likely to have given up the job on their own account and they are certainly likely to find employment much more quickly than older workers. The extent of unemployment among younger workers is, moreover, not so great as that of older workers nor does their unemployment last so long. The old unemployed worker is becoming one of the central tragic figures of increased automation. Statistics vary slightly from year to year but in general more than half of the men who are unemployed for a year or more at any one time are aged fifty-five to sixty-five. Sinfield's study of the unemployed in South Shields showed that the sense of despair and worthlessness is acute among this group of workers:[3] 'Older men often despaired, alternating between frantic search and lethargy. More often than others they said it was no good looking for work.' The situation is, of course, very similar in the United States for the same industrial processes and values are at work. Dorsey's study[4] of redundant workers tried to assess the comparative importance of various factors to the individual's ability to find employment and concluded that 'Among five variables tested for their relationship to re-employment—age, skill, sex and family status, education, and area of residence—age was quantitatively the most important as an explanation of the length of workers' frictional adjustment period.' The older workers' greater difficulty in finding employment is due partly to their greater reluctance to move away from their district, partly due to their lower educational qualifications, to the greater prevalence of disabilities of various forms and degrees and above all, perhaps, to the employers' general belief that they are less productive than younger workers.[5]

Skill is another obvious factor. Unskilled manual workers account for almost half of all men registered as unemployed. Viewed from a different angle, their unemployment rate is between seven and eight times higher than the unemployment rate of other men. Education is another factor though official statistics do not classify the unemployed in this way. The importance of education will increase in the future with increased automation. What will be needed in automated industries is not so much skill of the traditional kind but rather ability not only to do tasks well but also to train for new tasks as industrial processes become obsolete. The value of education is obvious in such situations. In Galbraith's words,[6] 'An aeronautical engineer, with the decline in demand for manned military aircraft, may have trouble finding employment in his speciality. But with a little training and some slight loss of dignity he becomes an excellent appliance salesman.' Though, true to the tradition of economists, he underestimates the human problems involved in redundancies, he is fundamentally right that an educated person will find it easier to adapt to industrial changes than an uneducated person.

Finally, unemployment varies from one region of the country to another. Despite the ups and downs of the national unemployment rate since the end of the last war and the changes in government employment policies with regard both to the whole country and to the regions separately, the comparative positions of the country's various regions in the unemployment league have remained the same. Northern Ireland, Scotland, Northern England, North-Western England and Wales have headed the table throughout the whole of this period with Ireland having by far the highest rates of unemployment. These higher unemployment rates must also be seen in the light of the large numbers of workers, particularly the young, who have emigrated from these regions to the more prosperous parts of the country.

The weakest groups of workers in terms of age, skill and education who are thought to be of least value to the industrial system are the most likely victims of unemployment. It is a gross over-simplification of real-life situations if these structural characteristics of the unemployed are seen individually and in isolation from one another rather than as an interacting and reinforcing group of factors. These inter-relationships are manifested in many ways but perhaps more than in any other way they are reflected in the length of unemployment. Table 7 shows that the proportion of the long-term unemployed—whether defined as those unemployed for over six months or over twelve months—was much higher in 1971 when the national unemployment rate was high than in 1966 when it was low. Moreover, the recent high unemployment was affecting more severely the weakest groups for they tend to be over-represented among the long-term unemployed. The unskilled, the disabled and the over fifty-five, especially if they live in the development areas, are much more likely to be long-term unemployed than other workers.

TABLE 7   *Length of unemployment for wholly unemployed men in Great Britain*

Weeks	October 1966	October 1971
	%	%
2 or less	26·5	14·3
2–8	27·7	23·5
8–26	21·1	29·3
26–52	9·5	14·5
52 or more	15·2	18·4

Source: Department of Employment *Gazettes.*

An unskilled unemployed worker who is over fifty-five and who lives in one of the development areas has very few, if any, chances of finding employment. We have already referred to the feelings of the older unemployed in Sinfield's study.[7] Ex-prisoners and ex-mental hospital patients in the same study felt that 'they were acceptable only for the roughest jobs with the least security and were the first victims of any lay-off: in this way they were kept on the margin of the labour force'.

It should also be borne in mind that, as the government's own surveys have shown, long-term unemployment is a handicap in itself to a person's chances of finding employment.[8] Government statistics underestimate the extent of long-term unemployment because they are based on the current spell of unemployment of those registered as unemployed. In this way a person who manages to get short spells of employment, though in effect suffers from long-term unemployment, may be registered among the short-term unemployed. In all these ways the industrial system militates against its own victims to create a large population group that is unwanted and stigmatized. In a competitive world where the survival of the fittest is the industrial pattern, the weak will not only suffer but they will suffer with the full knowledge and approval of society—or rather its industrial leaders—for their plight is seen as being either inevitable or the result of their own personal inadequacies.

Long-term unemployment, low pay and poverty are inter-related and they overlap even though not all the low-paid workers suffer from long-term unemployment and not all the low-paid workers are in poverty. This vicious circle that traps the industrially weak in poverty so tightly that they can hardly escape is the inevitable result of an industrial system which is primarily governed by the principle of maximization of profits. Workers are not considered as persons but as productive units to be discarded when they can no longer serve the financial interests of their employers. This functional relationship between employers and employees has remained fundamentally the same since the early days of industrialization even though other aspects of the work situation may have changed. The work place is safer and more pleasant physically now than it once was; employers are less authoritarian and they generally have to give notice to their employees before dismissal; there are welfare and personnel departments to make the relationship between employers and employees more trouble free and to improve employee's work performance; and there are the trade unions to protect the workers and to promote their interests. Fundamentally, however, a worker is a hired hand to perform certain duties for a certain financial reward, to be kept or dismissed depending on the firm's necessity

84

for his services and on his ability to perform his duties profitably to the employer in a competitive labour market.

The mass of statistics about the unemployed tends to over-shadow the effects of unemployment on the individual person who is unemployed. As the General Secretary of the Trade Union Congress recently remarked when discussing the variations in the national unemployment rate,[9] 'If you are unemployed you are not 2·5 per cent unemployed or 3·5 per cent unemployed—you are 100 per cent unemployed.' Unemployment should be seen as a personal problem first and as a national problem second. The individual unemployed can suffer economic, emotional and social hardship largely because of the emphasis which society places on the value of work and self-reliance. We shall be dealing with the financial problems of the unemployed later and here we shall refer to their other problems briefly only because they are obvious and well known. A person's job largely determines today not only his income but his status in the social structure. His relationships with his family, his friends and others are influenced by whether he works or not and by the job he does. Loss of job means loss of a basis from which one forms relationships with other people. It is, therefore, not unnatural that unemployment can make people feel insecure, depressed, resentful, apathetic, etc. After surveying over 100 research reports on unemployment in the 1930s, Eisenberg and Lazarfeld[10] suggested that the long-term unemployed pass successively through these six psychological stages: injury, fear and anger; apathy; quieting down and activity; futility; hopelessness and fear; acquiescence and apathy. Sinfield's more recent study found all but three of the unemployed in the sample were in poverty—using the Abel-Smith and Townsend standard—and that, 'The three effects of unemployment most commonly mentioned were depression, irritability and the problem of passing the time and these were often linked together.'[11] When unemployment hits a whole district because of sudden closure of firms its effects reverberate throughout the whole community. It 'can assume', writes Daniel,[12] 'the proportions of a natural disaster or alien invasion'.

Causes of unemployment

The recent government policies which were intentionally designed to increase the rate of unemployment lend support to our thesis that social security services and economic policy in general are always guided by the economic interests of the dominant classes in society. They show that the economic interests of employers and employees in a profit-oriented capitalist society are basically in conflict though this is not always clearly obvious. The post-war policy of co-operation between trade unions and employers is based on the principle of what Tawney called 'the balance of power' rather than on the principle of identity of interests. It is based on fear rather than on trust; on tactical compromises rather than on firm beliefs in the same principles. Such peace, Tawney remarked fifty years ago,[13] 'is precarious, insincere and short'. Rex had very much the same thing in mind when he suggested the concept of the 'truce situation' as a way of resolving the conflict between the classes in society. Leaders of conflicting classes realize that they have to compromise, to adopt a process of give and take, in order to avoid an all-out conflict that would be too costly to both sides. Such compromises can result in 'the emergence of a value system and of social institutions which are the social institutions of neither class, but belong to the truce situation itself'.[14] These 'truce situations', which are typical practices in a welfare state, create limited areas of co-operation between the classes and they last so long as the conditions of the truce are observed by both sides. They are inherently unstable because of the contradictory demands they make on the participants and 'could only become the basis of a new social order in exceptionally favourable conditions'.[15] Though Rex's thesis appears to contain contradictory lines of argument and it runs also the risk of mistaking temporary compromise by the conflicting groups as permanent adjustments in social class relationships, it can be useful in analysing individual social policy measures.

The abolition of subsistence poverty and the provision of 'full' employment are policies stemming from truce situations. The truce situation requires that the government should ensure that no one lives in subsistence poverty so long as certain conditions are observed by the poor. The moment the poor violate the conditions of the truce they can forfeit the whole or part of the benefits of the truce. Also the moment they try to extend the conditions of the truce by attempting to redefine poverty, for example, they will be resisted. Similarly, the truce situation on which full employment is based involves a number of conditions, a basic one of which is that the working class must not exploit the conditions of the prevailing labour market either by pressing for wages which are too high or by demanding the right to have a say in the running of industries. It is part of elementary economic theory that 'When unemployment is small, the bargaining position of unions is, in general, strong.'[16] Vice versa, 'Employers, on their side, will deem it wise under such circumstances to grant increases in wages.'[17] Employers can go on yielding to the demands of trade unions for high wages so long as they can pass on the extra cost, if any, to the consumers. This process cannot go on indefinitely, however, since goods will become uncompetitive in the international market. When this point is reached which clearly threatens the profits of the firm, then employers must feel that the conditions of the truce situation have been violated by the trade unions. Moreover, as Kalecki observed thirty years ago,[18] 'under a regime of permanent full employment, "the sack" would cease to play its role as a disciplinary measure. The social position of the boss would be undermined and the self-assurance and class consciousness of the working class would grow.' Employers, therefore, with the help of the government retaliate to reduce the strength of the trade unions and to return to the conditions of the truce situation or better still to conditions more favourable to themselves. This retaliation is, of course, presented as being necessary for the 'national interest'. It is argued that the trade unions, having become too powerful, are holding 'the community' to ransom; and that inflation undermines the interests of the whole country. Both these processes must be stopped by reducing the high growth of wages and by ridding industry of surplus labour.

We can now try to understand the recent rise in unemployment using the concepts of the 'balance of power' and the 'truce situation'. We said earlier that until 1966 it was generally thought that full employment existed in this country in spite of the prevalence of high unemployment rates in some of the country's regions. Even if we assume that regional unemployment can be eradicated and that full employment conditions can prevail in all parts of an industrial society, it does not obviously mean that unemployment can be abolished altogether. Some of the workers are bound to be dissatisfied with their jobs because of poor working conditions, low wages, unhappy personal relationships with others at work, etc., and will want to move to other jobs. This type of unemployment, however, is largely voluntary, it is of short duration, it affects comparatively small numbers of workers and it is to the benefit of the individual concerned as well as of the society in general.

It is not only voluntary unemployment that persists in a full employment society but structural unemployment as well. Structural unemployment is the inevitable consequence of the adaptation of the national economy to changing needs and circumstances. A number of factors bring about structural unemployment. Foreign competition, changes in consumers' tastes, exhaustion of raw materials, government taxation and tariff policies, technical changes or innovations in the production process and new management methods are the main factors contributing to structural unemployment. It is generally assumed that structural unemployment is in the 'national interest' for it benefits everybody. How true, however, is this? It is useful for our purposes to divide the factors contributing to structural unemployment into two groups: those factors which result in a decline in the availability or in the demand for the products of the firm irrespective of any change in the management or technology of the industry. Examples are the exhaustion of coal and its effects on the mining industry, people's preference for travel by car and its effects on the railways, the invention of television and its effects on the cinema industry, etc. These factors are usually beyond the control of management and the effects harm both the industrialists as well as the workers. The second group of factors is the result of decisions by management to introduce labour-saving methods of production or of organization. These factors result primarily in an improvement of the profits of the firm, to a lesser extent in the improvement of the wages of the employees who retain their jobs, but they certainly harm the workers who are made redundant.

If an industrial country wishes to continue increasing its economic wealth—and all industrial countries are determined to do this—then some structural unemployment is inevitable. What has gone wrong during the last five years is the volume of structural unemployment, the motives behind this high volume of unemployment and the inability of the government to stimulate industrial growth or other types of employment to provide employment for the displaced workers. Government policies not only encouraged *structual unemployment* but they also increased *cyclical or general unemployment*. Structural unemployment is 'the result of a poor adaptation of the worker's qualification and skills to need', while general unemployment is 'the result of a general shortage of demand'[19] for goods and services in the country. It is general unemployment that saps the strength of trade unions for while structural unemployment is of short-term duration, in conditions of general unemployment workers are out of work for very long periods. What were then the government policies that stepped up structural and general unemployment?

The first round of government activity that seems to have encouraged structural unemployment consisted of a group of social policy measures implemented in the mid-1960s which made it easier for employers to dismiss their workers and which made unemployment less unpalatable to the workers and the trade unions. There were four Acts passed one after the other in four consecutive years—the Contracts of Employment Act, 1963; the Industrial Training Act, 1964; the Redundancy Payments Act, 1965; and the National Insurance Act, 1966, which provided earnings-related benefits. These Acts were passed in the name of 'national interests' and they were supported by both political parties. Indeed the first two were passed by a Conservative government and the last two by a Labour government. The general discussion that accompanied this legislation coined new phrases that were considered more neutral, less emotional, more representative of a technological age. Words like unemployment and dismissal or sacking of workers gave way to words like redundancy, redeployment of labour, manpower policies, rationalization of labour, growth oriented policies, etc. The implication was that such changes were obviously necessary in the interests of technological growth and the financial interests of everybody in society. We shall discuss the effects of the National Insurance Act and the Redundancy Payments Act and leave discussion on the Industrial Training Act till the following section. The Contracts of Employment Act is insignificant in itself but as part of the quartet it reinforces the impression that unemployment and redundancies are inevitable, necessary for the benefit of all and that the State has done its best to lessen any adverse impact they may have on the workers.

It is not easy to isolate and measure the effects of these Acts on labour supply but the available evidence suggests that the introduction of better social security benefits has helped to increase unemployment. Thus Gujarati[20] suggests that an unintended consequence of the Redundancy Payments Act and the National Insurance Act 'may be an "artificial" increase in registered unemployment: an unemployed person is now under less pressure to look for a job immediately and may spend more time searching for a job'. He reached this tentative conclusion by comparing the number of unemployed persons with the number of unfilled vacancies during the years preceding and following these two Acts. He established that after 1966 these two indicators did not move as neatly in opposite directions as they did before 1966. He concedes that there may be other reasons for this besides the two Acts but feels that the trend is too clear to be sheerly coincidental. Contradicting Gujarati's suggestion is an unpublished government study conducted for the Department of Employment by the Government Social Survey which 'revealed that workers who got redundancy payments . . . took no longer to find a new job than workers who did not'.[21] The American study by Dorsey[22] which we referred to earlier in this chapter concluded that contrary to the general belief, a statistical examination 'of the relationship between the amount of separation pay and the length of frictional adjustment period . . . revealed no correlation between these two variables', even when such factors as age, skill, seniority, etc., were taken into account.

Perhaps the Redundancy Payments Act has been the most influential in affecting attitudes towards redundancies or to use the official language 'rationalization of labour'. The recent government study of this Act has shown that both employers and trade union officers felt that 'the Act has led to an increased flexibility and mobility of labour'.[23] In other words, it has become easier to discharge people from work since the Act. Moreover, it has been possible to do this with less industrial unrest. The incidence of strikes over redundancy has decreased since the Act while the incidence of strikes in general has been increasing.[24] This so-called increased flexibility of labour has affected the older and the sick workers more than the other workers. Again to put this in simpler words, rationalization of labour means sacking the old and the not so healthy and replacing them with the young and the healthy. The traditional trade union policy of 'first in, last out' has given way to a principle which is more likely to maximize economic growth and profits even though its justification in terms of justice and fairness to the individuals concerned is very doubtful.

The effects of these four pieces of legislation on the 'rationalization of labour' were not, however, so substantial as to undermine the bargaining position of the trade unions with the result that they could still secure rises in wages for their members which were thought by employers and the government to be inflationary since employers continued increasing their prices rather than reducing their profits. Various schemes of a voluntary and statutory nature were tried by the Labour government to stem the rise not of profits but in prices and particularly the rise in wages but with little success. Thus the spiral of inflation—higher prices leading to higher wages and higher wages leading to higher prices—

continued. The failure of these prices and incomes policies led the Labour government first, and then the Conservative government, to deflate demand in the economy, thus creating massive unemployment and thus hoping to reduce wage rises. The difference between the policies of the two governments is a matter of degree. The deflationary measures of the Conservative government until the summer of 1971 were larger and more ruthlessly pursued than those of the Labour government.

What were the methods used by both governments to deflate demand in the economy? First, by ensuring large budget surpluses. Such surpluses reduce demand in the economy either because they involve reductions in public expenditure or because they reduce the amount of income people have to spend through increased direct or indirect taxation. In other words the government reduced its own expenditure and forced people through taxation to reduce their expenditure with the result that demand in the economy was also reduced. Second, the government not only reduced its expenditure but it also forced the nationalized industries to reduce their capital expenditure so that expansion of employment suffered. Third, the supply of money was made more difficult and interest rates on loans were increased with the result that private companies either found it more difficult to expand or cut down expansion programmes. Finally, the Conservative government threw its weight behind employers in an attempt to beat demands for a high rise in wages.[25]

This massive deflation of demand for goods and services in the community inevitably meant that employers had to reduce their labour force thus increasing the national rate of unemployment from 2·7 per cent in January 1970 to 4·3 per cent in January 1972. Moreover, many firms who made workers redundant have found that they can achieve the same production with fewer men by re-organizing their existing labour force, by using overtime work and so on. The automation of the industrial processes has been gaining ground during the last decade and the deflation of demand provided an excellent opportunity to employers to reduce their labour force in a short period of time. In all these ways the bargaining strength of the trade unions for higher wages has theoretically been reduced while that of the employers has been improved.

It is worth pointing out that if the social security measures of the mid-1960s coupled with the Industrial Relations Act have strengthened the employers' bargaining position, the payment of supplementary benefit to the families of strikers may have had the effect of strengthening the position of trade unions and thus making it more difficult for employers to force workers to accept low increases in wages. This helps to explain the persistent demands in the Conservative Party that the government should tackle the 'scandal' of subsidizing strikes through public funds. On the surface, it appears that the truce situation we talked about earlier has been temporarily redefined in favour of employers so that the full employment of the future may not mean the same as the full employment situation of the 1950s and early 1960s. It may legitimize the acceptance of higher unemployment rates as necessary to the national interest. There are already signs of economists considering an unemployment rate that is not so low as that of the 1950s and not so high as the present, desirable for the country in the future. Thus Day writes that,[26] 'it is now pretty clear that if we are to maintain our mixed economy and avoid intolerable inflation, the unemployment percentage cannot be allowed to fall to levels as low as those we enjoyed in the fifties and sixties'. Recently, however, there have been several industrial conflicts where new forms of radical action by workers have reversed important decisions taken by employers and the government. This new radicalism, if it persists, can change the whole balance of power between employers and workers.

Government services for the unemployed

Apart from the fiscal policies used by governments to increase demand in the community and to encourage economic growth and industrial expansion so as to reduce the level of unemployment in general, there are also three services with a more social, personal character which we discuss below. The reflation of the economy consists of measures more or less opposite to those we referred to briefly for the recent deflationary policies of the two governments. The inflation and deflation of the economy are primarily the concern of the economists while the three measures we discuss below are of equal concern to the students of both economics and social administration. These three social policy measures concern regional unemployment, the retraining of workers and the employment services.

We are not concerned here with the details of government policies towards the development areas but rather with the principles and also to note that decisions by industrialists affect the lives of people as much, and in this case more, than decisions by governments. Industrialists have naturally been inclined to start businesses in areas which they have thought more advantageous to their financial interests. Governments, both Labour and Conservative, have adopted the line that this is inevitable and desirable in a capitalist society and they have tried to alleviate the ill effects of this policy mainly by offering financial inducements to industrialists to move their businesses to the development areas and to a lesser extent by giving meagre financial assistance to some of the workers who emigrate from such areas to take up jobs in the more prosperous regions. Whether the policy of attracting industry to development areas through government efforts has succeeded or failed depends on one's criteria. It is impossible to prove success or failure in the strict sense of these words. In the first place, regions of high unemployment suffer more from geographical mobility than the rest of the country with the result that when their unemployment rates fall it is difficult to know exactly what proportion of this reduction is due to emigration and what proportion to the provision of better job opportunities in the region as a result of government policies. When government policies succeed in attracting industries to these regions, the volume of emigration falls and in this way the effect of government measures on unemployment reduction is underestimated. Second, many of the new jobs created by the industries attracted to development areas by government policies are for married women who would not otherwise have gone out to work. In this way the unemployment rate may not be affected even though more people in the region are at work. Third, even if the relative severity of unemployment in the development regions *vis-à-vis* that of the rest of the country shows no improvement, it is difficult to deduce that government policies were a failure because the position of the regions could have worsened without government aid. There is evidence to suggest that when unemployment rises in the country, regions of high unemployment suffer most. Cairncross's[27] review of the effectiveness of regional policies led her to the conclusion, which is generally shared, that 'the Development Areas have almost, but not quite, held their own against the breakneck rundown of their older industries. The number of jobs has been virtually stagnant, but workers have been shifted on an impressive scale out of a few declining industries and into a much wider range of newer ones.'

There are very good economic reasons why governments have decided to emphasize more the policy of encouraging industry relocation than the policy of encouraging people through substantial financial inducements to move out of development areas. The high population density of the more prosperous areas would have made it impossible to absorb large numbers of immigrants without severe strains on the physical environment. Public services such as transport, schools, hospitals and above all houses would have to be substantially expanded at a high cost while such facilities would be left to wither in the development areas. There are also social grounds against excessive labour geographical mobility—the preservation of local communities because of their cultural heritage and the prevention of possible psychological ill-effects on people who are indirectly forced to emigrate. Zarka's[28] examination of this question in Western Europe led him to the conclusion, which I thoroughly share, that geographical mobility of labour 'should be regarded as a palliative. It is the responsibility of the public authorities to endeavour in the first place to bring capital to the places where people have their homes.' To this one can also add that if governments cannot convince industrialists to move to the development areas, then they should be prepared to start industries themselves in such areas. Most economists and politicians are agreed that increased state intervention in industry is the only way to curb unemployment in capitalist societies. Thus Brown's[29] examination of the causes of the recent high unemployment rates led him to the conclusion that 'full employment can only in the present stage of capitalist development be even attempted by extending state ownership as well as by extending state provision.' Jenkins[30] concludes that regional unemployment 'will not be cured without more direct Government involvement and a greater use of public enterprise'.

Regional unemployment involves more than economic considerations. It is also a problem of excessive centralization of government with the result that few, if any, important government decisions are made in the regions themselves. Politically, culturally and economically the regions of high unemployment have been neglected and it needs a concerted effort on all three fronts to improve their position substantially.

The Industrial Training Act, 1964, set up Industrial Training Boards which impose a levy upon all employers and make grants to those employers who undertake training schemes. Most of the training of workers is thus conducted by private industry. The government, however, runs its own retraining centres, numbering fifty-two and providing 13,000 places for unemployed workers wanting to be retrained. So far, government training centres have not had much impact on the labour market for three main reasons. First, the idea of retraining is an alien notion to the public. As Daniel has said,[31] 'retraining is seen as something abnormal, undertaken only by abnormal people, people who have something wrong with them. It is viewed more as industrial rehabilitation for the handicapped than as a normal activity for normal people'. Second, retraining does not guarantee a man a job though naturally every effort is made by the officers of the training centres to find him a job. During periods of high unemployment, when retraining is most necessary, it is that much more difficult to find the right type of employment in the applicant's area. Retraining is useful and necessary but it can only be of real value if there are the right kind of jobs in the right areas to be filled by the newly trained. Finally, training centres are few in number and consequently they are inconvenient for people living a long distance from them. The inadequacy of the provision of training centres is perhaps highlighted by the fact that the country spends about five times more on redundancy payments as compensation to redundant workers than on the government training scheme. The government has recently announced new measures to expand the scope of the retraining centres. Since both political parties are agreed on the value of this service, its substantial expansion in the near future is more than probable. Its contribution to the reduction of unemployment depends on the existence of a low level of unemployment, on the payment of adequate grants to the retrained workers and, where it involves geographical mobility, on the existence of adequate housing. It is generally agreed that the existing housing shortage is a strong deterrent to mobility. Shanks,[32] considering this problem, suggested the establishment of 'a special Government Housing Corporation to build houses for letting in areas to which new workers are to be attracted, and to buy up houses in declining areas' belonging to workers who decide to move.

Various studies have shown that the regional and local offices of the Department of Employment play a minor role in helping people to find employment. It is estimated that the local employment offices find jobs for one-fifth to one-quarter of all persons finding jobs in any one year. The proportion of redundant workers helped by these offices to find employment is even smaller. Kahn's follow-up survey of a group of workers made redundant in 1957 showed that only 15 per cent had found their first job through the employment exchange.[33] The government's own study of the Redundancy Payments Act, fourteen years later, showed that despite all the improvements the employment exchanges had gone through, they placed the same proportion of redundant workers. There are three main explanations for this poor performance of the employment exchanges. The first is their poor public image. From their beginning in 1909 and through the mass unemployment of the 1930s, employment exchanges have been associated with the payment of unemployment benefit or assistance to the unemployed. Reid's recent study[34] showed that nearly half of a sample of redundant workers agreed that the employment exchange was mainly 'a place for layabouts' or a 'place where you collect dole'. The result of this poor image has been that employers do not notify the Department of Employment of vacancies in good jobs and, vice versa, skilled and professional unemployed persons do not approach the employment exchanges for help. It is this reinforcing vicious circle which governments have been trying, rather half-heartedly, to break. Thus a register of professional jobs has been compiled, schemes for the payment of unemployment benefit through the post have been experimentally used and recently the government decided to separate the administration of unemployment benefits from the employment service.[35] What governments have not done is the one thing that would, more than anything else, give employment exchanges a central role in job placing—this is to require all employers to notify vacancies to the employment exchanges. It is not any more of an undue interference with employers' freedom than the fact that employers have to pay insurance contributions for their employees, to pay redundancy allowances, to give notice before dismissal, to observe safety standards, and so on. The second reason for the poor performance of employment exchanges is the low standard of their premises and their staff. As a *New Society* editorial said,[36] 'Labour exchanges are dingy, depressing and inconveniently located. The service is under-financed and under-staffed. The staff lack the time, skills and training to do anything other than a clerical task.' This picture is not confined to the employment exchanges: it applies to a lesser or greater extent to the supplementary benefit offices and the national insurance offices. It is a reflection of the philosophy of private affluence and public squalor. So long as this philosophy is accepted, governments will continue making plans for the modernization and professionalization of services that are necessary for the working class but without ever implementing them. The third reason is the working-class culture which encourages job finding through the informal systems of kinship and friendship. This is particularly true of homogeneous communities but it also applies to heterogeneous communities. In part this is a reflection of the insecurity of the working class in the employment structure and in part a reflection of the inadequacies of the government employment services. Until governments accept the principle that job finding is a government responsibility, a public service and not an industry to be shared with the private sector, employment exchanges will not shed their present discredited image. One cannot but agree with the pessimistic editorial of *New Society*[37] that, taking into account government thinking so far, 'the pattern that seems most likely to develop is as follows: private commercial agencies creaming off the best jobs and the best applicants; private charitable agencies struggling to cope with the socially disadvantaged, such as the redundant executive, the older worker, and the blacks; and the public service bumbling along much as it is'.

The general assumption in official and lay circles so far has been that governments should be concerned primarily with measures to reduce unemployment rather than with measures to improve the quality and the value of work to people. We referred in the last chapter to the governments' emphasis on industrial growth and the neglect of how the produce of this growth should be distributed. A similar misplacement of emphasis is taking place in the field of employment. Governments are primarily concerned that people should be at work, physically safe work, rather than whether work has any real meaning or gives any personal satisfaction to the people or has any value to society. All the schemes we discussed in this section, if improved substantially, will ensure that unemployment is reduced but they will do little to alter the conclusion of most sociological studies that a large proportion of the industrial working class find 'that their work is monotonous, that their job does not absorb their full attention, and that the pace of their work is too fast'.[38] Radical suggestions like the professionalization of labour[39] or the control of industry by workers[40] or the subordination of the industrial system to the needs of the people rather than vice versa are considered Utopian for they are contrary to the dominant social values that serve the interests of the upper classes well. Yet public demands for improvements in the personal and social aspects of the workplace are likely to increase in the future as more people face up to the fact that their work does not give them enough or any personal satisfaction. Like the demand for equality in pay we discussed in the last chapter, the demand for the professionalization and democratization of work will come slowly and gradually. Drawing a parallel between the physical hazards and the boredom and uncreativeness of work, Parker[41] felt that, 'If the achievements of the past fifty years were concentrated on the physical environment of work, attention over the next fifty years must turn increasingly to the quality of working life itself—the social relationship of work and the opportunities it gives for personal fulfilment.' To this we can only add that increased professionalization and increased participation at work will tend to be accompanied by demands for increased equality in economic rewards, because greater equality in one aspect of life cannot but have repercussions in a similar direction in other aspects.

Social security benefits for the unemployed

There are two social security benefits specifically for the unemployed—redundancy payments and unemployment benefits. Redundancy payments are lump sums, financed from employers' contributions, and paid to all redundant workers above the age of eighteen who have been with the same employer for at least two years prior to the redundancy.[42] They are not an insurance benefit not do they take into account the financial or family responsibilities of the redundant worker.

Three main arguments were put forward for the scheme of redundancy payments. First that a redundant worker suffers social and economic hardship and a lump sum paid to him will help to reduce some of the social and economic hardship which he suffers. Second, compensation for loss of job will reduce workers' opposition to technical or management changes that lead to redundancies. We have already referred to this and pointed out that by and large the Act has achieved this aim. Third, that a worker has a right to his job and that it is right and proper that he should be compensated when his job disappears through no fault of his own. Put in this way it sounds a moral argument. A more pedestrian, but perhaps a more honest way of expressing this is that technical change benefits the employers most, the non-redundant workers to a lesser extent, and it is therefore right to pay some compensation to those workers who lose their jobs in the process. Being a moral argument, this can neither be proved nor disproved. So we shall instead concentrate on the first argument, i.e. whether involuntary redundancy causes social and economic hardship and if so whether the Redundancy Act relieves this hardship.

It can be argued that all job changes, whether voluntary or involuntary, involve some social and economic hardship and that therefore redundant workers receive preferential treatment. This argument does not stand up to much criticism for voluntary job changes normally involve an improvement in the person's occupation or income or status or in all three. This is not necessarily true of redundancies. The government survey[43] compared the costs incurred as a result of changing jobs by redundant workers and by non-redundant workers and established that 'redundant workers tended to lose income, pension rights, fringe benefits and job satisfaction as consequence of changing jobs. On the other hand, those non-redundant workers in the sample who changed jobs voluntarily generally gained in all these respects.'

Obviously any lump sum paid to a redundant worker will be useful but the question is whether the criteria used by the Redundancy Act in deciding the amount of the lump sum are the right ones. In other words do those who suffer most from redundancies also get the largest sums in redundancy allowances ? The amount of compensation paid by the Act was based on the assumption that the extent of the social and economic costs suffered by the redundant worker are related to his age, length of service with the same employer and his earnings. Thus the older the worker, the longer his service with the same employer and the higher his earnings, the larger the amount he will receive in redundancy payment.[44] The government survey confirmed the conclusion reached by previous research on redundancy that the main factor which determines the extent of hardship following redundancy is old age. In the words of Kahn,[45]

> Age was a distinct handicap after discharge, while skill was not the golden key that opened all doors irrespective of other considerations. Though skill was no doubt of help in securing employment, and while age was not an insuperable obstacle, as a broad generalization it was youth rather than skill which was an asset after redundancy.

The government survey also showed that the other two factors— years of employment with the same firm and amount of earnings— were relevant to some extent but not so important. The length of service with the same employer was generally connected with the worker's age and as such was a relevant criterion. The amount of earnings is a relevant factor only if one accepts the notion of relative poverty which we referred to in the case of earnings-related benefits. The authors of the survey felt justified in concluding that the criteria used by the Redundancy Payments Act to determine the amount of the payment are the right ones. Though the criteria used by the Act are broadly relevant, it does not mean that the hardest hit received the largest sums in compensation for there are other criteria which the Act does not take into account and which the researchers did not investigate. It does not take into account family responsibilities, local unemployment rate, skills and so on. One cannot but agree with Wedderburn's[46] conclusion that a redundancy payment is 'an indiscriminate way of minimizing hardship'.

Above all it is a mistake to conclude that the Redundancy Payments Act has done away with the social and economic ill-effects which redundancy has on the individuals concerned. It has made redundancy slightly less unbearable for the redundant workers and it also pays the largest sums to those groups of workers whom the Act itself has made more vulnerable to redundancy. It has not done anything to combat the ill-effects of redundancy on the occupational status of redundant employees nor has it solved the psychological problems which redundancy brings to the individual and his family. Thus only 31 per cent of redundant senior managers in the government survey found comparable jobs and the remaining 69 per cent took jobs at a lower level—18 per cent of them had to be satisfied with unskilled manual jobs. At the other end of the occupational scale, 42 per cent of semi-skilled workers found similar jobs while another 42 per cent had to take unskilled jobs. Generally, then, redundancy for most people means a drop on the occupational ladder or permanent unemployment. The payment of a small sum of money does not compensate for all the losses involved in redundancy. Thus 66 per cent of those who received redundancy pay in the government survey would prefer to be in their old job. Though a small sum of money is always welcome, the only meaningful compensation for redundancy is a new job that is just as good, or preferably better, than the old job. The Redundancy Payments Act provides a sugar coating to a bitter experience; it does not improve a person's position in the occupational or class structure. To say that redundancies are in 'the national interest' is only another way of saying that they are in the interests mainly of employers and to a much smaller extent of those workers who don't lose their jobs.

But since most workers will suffer from unemployment or redundancy sometime in their working life it means that what they gain in some periods of their working life, they will more than lose in others.

The second social security benefit for the unemployed is unemployment benefit payable to those employees who have paid the necessary number of insurance contributions. Since 1966 all the unemployed who qualify for unemployment benefit will receive a flat rate benefit for themselves and their families up to a period of twelve months and an earnings-related supplement up to a period of six months. There is no doubt about the intentions of Parliament with regard to the earnings-related supplement: it was designed to make short-term unemployment more acceptable and to encourage the unemployed to return to work as soon as possible and certainly not later than six months. It was primarily concerned with industrial growth and secondarily only with the welfare of the unemployed. As we mentioned earlier, the paradox of the existing system is that it provides higher benefits for the short-term unemployed whose needs in terms of replacement of clothing, furniture and so on are lower than those of the long-term unemployed. The flat rate unemployment benefit is paid for twelve months only because it was felt that most unemployed would be able to find employment within that period and that those who remain unemployed after that can do with a sharp reminder from the State that it is about time they went back to work. Both of these notions are mistaken. As Table 7 showed, almost one in five of unemployed men has been out of work for twelve months or more. The proportion is higher among the older workers, the unskilled and those living in areas of high unemployment. These characteristics of the long-term unemployed are structural and they are beyond their control. The recommendation of the Beveridge Report was that unemployment benefit should be paid for as long as unemployment lasts (in the same way that sickness is paid for as long as sickness lasts) and that the unemployed should be encouraged to accept retraining. A change in the existing regulations in this direction, coupled with the new enthusiasm of the government for retraining, will be a step in the right direction and will not involve any significant rise in expenditure.

Not all the unemployed who satisfy the insurance contribution conditions will receive unemployment benefit. There are a number of other conditions which have to be satisfied first. Thus unemployment benefit may be refused for a period of six weeks if it is decided that the unemployed worker left his job voluntarily without good reason; if he was dismissed because of his misconduct; if he refuses, without good cause, to look for a job and to accept offers of jobs or industrial training. These are all vague requirements and their interpretation rests with the insurance officers. As we have mentioned several times so far, the unemployed are a discredited group in society and it is natural that insurance officers, especially since they are not trained in any branch of the behavioural sciences, will reflect these attitudes to a lesser or greater extent and thus discriminate against the unemployed. As we shall see in the following paragraphs they are tacitly encouraged in this by the whole ethos of the host of official regulations for the unemployed. Sinfield refers to these problems in his study.[47] He found that the distinction between voluntary and involuntary unemployment 'was often a shadowy and arbitrary one'. As for the rule that the unemployed must prove that they are looking for a job he reached the conclusion that, 'In an area of high unemployment there was no way of testing a man's declared willingness to work; because of the large element of chance and the role of the family and friends, finding work was no indication of the intensity of the search.'[48]

TABLE 8   *Distribution of total registered unemployed with regard to social security benefits, November* 1970, *Great Britain*

	%
Flat rate unemployment benefit only	25
Flat rate and earnings-related benefit	16
Flat rate benefit and supplementary benefit	9
Flat rate, earnings-related benefit and supplementary benefit	1
Supplementary benefit only	24
No benefit of any kind	26

Source: Central Statistical Office, *Social Trends*, No. 2, HMSO, 1971, p. 86.

Table 8 shows that half the unemployed do not qualify for an insurance benefit. Though this must be partly due to the fact that some of the registered unemployed are married women who do not usually pay contributions and are therefore not entitled to unemployment benefit, the proportion is still too high. The corresponding proportion for retirement pensions for men is only 1·6 per cent. Without further details it is not possible to explain this breakdown of the insurance principle. During periods of low unemployment it can be argued that the unemployed are marginal workers who move from job to job and do not, therefore, have a satisfactory insurance record. During periods of high unemployment it can be argued that marginal workers are joined by those of the unemployed who have been out of work for more than twelve months and have thus exhausted their right to unemployment benefit. Whatever the explanation it is clearly an unsatisfactory state of affairs. It was not the intention of the Beveridge Report or of the policy-makers in 1946 that half the unemployed should fall through the net of the insurance scheme.

Like all other persons whose income from work stops, the unemployed are entitled to apply for supplementary benefit because their insurance benefit does not cover rent, or because they are not entitled to, or have exhausted, their right to an insurance benefit. Whether they are granted supplementary benefit will depend on their circumstances but, apart from married women who are the financial responsibility of their husbands, it is difficult to believe that there are many unemployed over twelve months with financial resources to disqualify them from receiving supplementary benefit. Similarly, those who do not qualify for an insurance benefit in the first place are usually men of irregular work who would not have any financial resources. Thus many of the unemployed receive supplementary benefit and as Table 8 shows almost a quarter of them rely exclusively on supplementary benefit. The other quarter of the unemployed who receive no social security benefit of any kind must be married women, young workers under sixteen and the officially designated 'work-shy'.

In areas in which job opportunities are considered adequate by the supplementary benefits commission, unemployed men under the age of forty-five who are single, fit and unskilled and who apply for supplementary benefit are paid an allowance for four weeks only and are told that the benefit will be stopped after that. If at the end of the four weeks the unemployed man does not re-apply for supplementary benefit, the allowance is stopped. If he re-applies, he has to satisfy the supplementary benefit officer that he has made a genuine effort to find employment, otherwise the benefit is paid at a reduced rate until he appeals to the supplementary benefit tribunal. The vast majority, 97 per cent, do not re-apply after the end of the four weeks but of those who do, the majority receive the full benefit. Less stringent regulations apply to the skilled, the married, the older worker and the not so physically fit. Unemployed men who are skilled and those who have dependants are subjected to a three-months' rule, instead of four weeks'. Unemployed over the age of forty-five and those who are not physically fit are subjected to a six-months' rule.

The similarity between these rules and those of the old poor law about the 'able-bodied pauper' are apparent. It has always been felt that the young and physically fit unemployed are potentially worse malingerers than other unemployed workers and they have always been dealt with more harshly by the social security system. Apart from the doubtful validity of this assumption, all these rulings are blatantly discriminatory on two counts: first, many people are not aware of their rights and, of those who are, many are not prepared to take their cases to official tribunals. Second, the adequacy of job opportunities, which is the basic criterion for the enforcement of these rules, is determined not by the number of vacant jobs notified to the local employment exchanges but rather by whether the Department of Employment feels that there are adequate job opportunities. The net result of these rulings is that at least 90,000 unemployed lose their supplementary benefit every year and others are paid reduced benefits. The amount which the state saves is insignificant but the hardship inflicted on individual people can be enormous.[49]

The other main indignity and injustice which the unemployed who apply for supplementary benefit suffer is through the wages stop rule. The aim of the 'wages stop' according to a Government Report[50] 'is to ensure that an unemployed man's income is *no greater* than it would be if he were in full-time employment'. The Supplementary Benefits Commission refuses to accept that the wages stop is a cause of family poverty; rather, 'it is a harsh reflection of the fact that there are many men in work living on incomes below the Supplementary Benefit standard'.[51] The Report on the wages stop is typical of recent reports on social security in the sense that though it is written in understanding, restrained language, its recommendations are still in line with nineteenth-century principles on poverty. It does not condemn or abuse the poor as the nineteenth-century government reports did; in fact it understands their plight but regretfully it recommends that they should stay poor. As Baroness Wootton has said when comparing the Beveridge Report with the Report of the Poor Law Commissioners in 1834,[52] though 'we do not any longer talk in this way, we do not act so very differently. The voice may be the voice of Beveridge in 1942; but the deeds are remarkably close to those of the Commissioners of 1834.' Clearly two social values are in conflict in the case of the wages stop—the value that no one should live in subsistence poverty and the value which society places on work. In this conflict, the value placed on work wins for it is felt that if the poor received more in supplementary benefit than in earnings, they would not be anxious to return to work. This is obviously a modified version of the principle of less eligibility which was the main feature of the poor law system from the eighteenth century onwards. It affected over 33,000 persons in 1970 of whom the vast majority were unemployed and the remaining few were mainly temporarily sick.

The introduction of the Family Income Supplement should have reduced the incidence of wage-stopped families by the fact that it increased the income of families at work which is considered necessary by the government. The decision whether an unemployed person should be wage-stopped and by how much is to some extent a subjective decision based on the views and feelings of the supplementary benefit officer about work, health, regular wages, malingering, poverty, morality and so on. Sinfield's assessment of the attitudes of supplementary benefit officers towards the unemployed is pertinent here:[53]

> Officers often seemed more anxious that they should not be taken in by a hard-luck story than that they should fail to meet any genuine need. In dealing with the unemployed the wide discretionary powers of the officers seemed to be most often exercised towards refusing or reducing assistance grants rather than adding to them or making special grants'.

It may be true that the hard line which the supplementary benefit officers take towards the so-called voluntary unemployed is a reflection of prevalent public attitudes. On the other hand, it is equally true that special 'drives' or special programmes to deal with this group may intensify public feeling towards the group. Social policy not only reflects but it also affects public attitudes.[54]

We know very little about the characteristics and living conditions of this group except what emerges from a government Report on fifty-two wage-stopped families in 1967[55] and a smaller study of eighteen families by the Child Poverty Action Group in 1972.[56] The Government Report paints a grim and harrowing picture of these families. Most of the fathers were long-term unemployed, of unskilled occupations, in poor health and one-third were registered disabled persons. The Report expressed doubts 'whether the men who suffered from the worst health or the greatest disability should have been regarded as being in the employment field at all'. In other words they should not have been wage-stopped since they were not fit to choose between working and not working. The standard of diet was poor with 'bread and potatoes . . . often eaten in large quantities' while 'fresh meat was bought only at weekends in many cases'. The standard of clothing was equally poor and children's shoes 'obviously a difficulty'; stocks of bed clothes were low and sometimes 'almost non-existent'. Half the families were in arrears with their rent, one-third had had their electricity or gas cut off at some time in the past, and a quarter 'ran short of fuel during the winter'. Two-thirds had had no holidays for five years and 'some said they had never had a holiday and never expected to'. Many children had no pocket money, many mothers were unable to have their hair done and television 'was often the only source of entertainment'. The Report summed up coolly the condition of these families as follows: 'The general impression derived from the visits was not so much one of grinding poverty in any absolute sense as one of unrelieved dreariness with, in some cases, little hope of improvement in the future.'[57] The Report made several recommendations designed to ensure that 'claimants who are subject to the wage stop are dealt with as sympathetically and equitably as possible'.[58] The study by the Child Poverty Action Group suggests, bearing in mind the smallness and the biased nature of the sample, that this hope for a sympathetic administration of the wages stop remains unfulfilled. Only four of the eighteen wage-stopped had the rule explained to them by the supplementary benefit officer and most of the wage-stopped had not even realized that they were being wage-stopped until they appraoched the Child Poverty Action Group for advice. There was a strong tendency for supplementary benefit officers to treat the wage-stopped as labourers without much serious attempt to find out what the man's potential earnings were. As regards the living conditions of the wage-stopped, the two reports reinforce each other in painting the same grim picture of severe hardship and strain.

Those who believe that the abolition of at least subsistence poverty is a fundamental duty of the government will want to see the wage-stop rule abolished. Similarly, those who believe that one of the basic characteristics of social policy must be the protection of the weak and the levelling up of the living standards of the poor will also wish the wage stop abolished. Also, those who know from experience that the administration of the wage stop rule is not only complicated but inherently punitive for it reflects some of society's hardest attitudes, cannot but argue for the abolition of the wage stop. Those who believe that the abolition of the wage stop will undermine work incentives, and those who believe that if people at work live in subsistence poverty they should, as a matter of principle, also live in the same condition when not at work, will defend the wage stop as necessary. Apart from moral arguments, however, what evidence is there that a small extra amount of money a week will affect a person's decision whether to go out to work or whether to stay at home? Several government statistical reports have classified small groups of unemployed people (varying from 5 per cent to 9 per cent of all all the registered unemployed) as 'work-shy' or 'voluntary unemployed' but these categorizations were based on the subjective assessment of the supplementary benefit officers.[59] These statistical reports merely tell us what the officers who have to find jobs for the unemployed think of their clients. They are not based on any medical, psychological or even plain survey evidence. It is a totally unsatisfactory situation that governments have been prepared to penalize people in poverty on pure assumptions without any real attempt to test the validity of their assumptions.

Goldthorpe and Lockwood and their associates[60] distinguished between 'instrumental' and 'solidaristic' attitude to work. An 'instrumental' attitude sees work as a means to an end and denotes no social commitment to the workplace, the employer or the other workers. A 'solidaristic' attitude sees work as a group activity and it involves loyalty to the firm and to the other workers. Hill, discussing unemployment in the context of Goldthorpe's and Lockwood's framework,[61] argues that a low-paid worker with an 'instrumental' view to work, may avoid work when things get on top of him at home. A low-paid worker, however, with a 'solidaristic' orientation to work may avoid work when he enjoys similar relationships with people not at work. In other words, the first type of worker will not bother to go to work while the second type will positively avoid it. Hill's conclusion is that 'Probably most of the apparently "voluntary" unemployed will have the "instrumental" view, but will have become discouraged and apathetic. But some, undoubtedly, may take the "solidaristic" view involving positively avoiding work.' Interesting though this hypothesis is, it needs verification. Nevertheless this approach is very important. What we should be asking ourselves is not why do some workers prefer to draw supplementary benefit and stay at home rather than work long hours in usually unpleasant and boring conditions for a low wage but rather why do so many low-paid workers decide to remain at work when they would have got just as much in social security benefit if they stayed at home. This line of thinking raises the question not only of abolishing the wage stop—which is an anachronism in a civilized society—but also the question of equality of incomes from work, the satisfaction which work provides or should provide, participation in decisions affecting work situations and other similar important issues. The wage-stopped unemployed workers merely point out the weaknesses of the existing systems of work and rewards from work. Society may use them as scapegoats—like it uses other minority groups such as immigrants—for its ills whereas in fact they are symptoms and victims of the social system. The wage-stopped should be a constant reminder to society that not only the social security system but the work and income systems as well are in dire need of reform.

5

∽∽∽∽∽∽∽∽∽∽∽∽

Old age and
social security

∽∽∽∽∽∽∽∽∽∽∽∽

The presence of large numbers of elderly retired people in the community is a comparatively recent phenomenon and society has not yet been able to make satisfactory accommodations to this fact. While the aged—men aged sixty-five and over and women aged sixty and over—constituted 4 per cent of the total population of Great Britain in 1851, the proportion increased by four times to 16·1 per cent by 1971, i.e. 8,761,000 elderly. This rise in the proportion of the elderly, due mostly to declining birth rates and partly to increased life expectancy,[1] is an achievement rather than a calamity for society. It is not the proportion of the elderly in the community as such that constitutes a social problem but 'rather the lag in adapting social institutions to the needs of older people without disrupting the machinery of the whole society'.[2] The social problem of old age is manifested in two inter-related ways: first, the concern by the elderly themselves about how to cope with their social, economic and other problems and second, the concern by society in general about how the presence of the elderly affects the economic and social structure of society. In this chapter we are primarily concerned with the economic situation of the elderly and with society's response to this.

The retirement role

Retirement from work is a new phenomenon, almost concurrent with industrialization. In pre-industrial societies, there was no period in one's life which was generally recognized as retirement nor were there any social policies for retirement. Old people were still economically dependent on the rest of society because of ill-health, absence of work opportunities, etc., but society did not accept as a matter of principle that the elderly had a right to give up work and that the younger generation had a duty to support the elderly. The changes in the economic, social and political systems that accompanied industrialization were responsible for the initiation of the role of retirement, i.e. the idea that people are perhaps entitled to give up work at a certain age and the younger sections of society have a duty to provide them with financial and other support through government administered services.[3] Traditional roles, however, do not disappear overnight nor do new roles become institutionalized so quickly. There is a transitory stage when both traditional and new roles co-exist, a stage of confusion, contradiction and conflict but which gradually clarifies the issues involved with the result that the old role expectations are abandoned and the new ones adopted by society.

The actual age at which retirement commences is a matter of conjecture and is determined by economic and political considerations rather than by any strict reference to the health conditions of the elderly. There is no one year in a lifetime when people's ability to work ceases or changes drastically and which can mark the beginning of retirement. Ageing is normally a gradual process which begins early in middle life and continues till late in old life. The minimum retirement age for men in this country was fixed at seventy in 1908 largely because of the economic costs of providing pensions. Since pensions were non-contributory it meant that they had to be paid out of government funds which at that stage of the country's economic development were provided mainly from the incomes of the middle and upper classes. In theory, as Gerig points out,[4] with the existence of surplus labour the government may decide on either a high retirement age to reduce the costs of pensions or on a low retirement age to improve the employment chances of younger workers. In practice, however, since the interests of the upper classes dominate social policy, particularly at the early stages of industrialization when pensions are usually introduced, it is the first alternative that is usually adopted. As the working classes secure more political power they tend to use it to lower the age of retirement. It is nevertheless difficult to change the age of retirement because once it is established it becomes part of the national culture with direct and indirect effects on the country's economic and social systems.[5] The retirement age for men in this country was lowered to sixty-five when the contributory insurance scheme was introduced in 1925 while the retirement age for women was fixed at sixty and they have both remained the same in spite of all the economic and social changes that have since taken place.

Not only are there more elderly in the community today than in the past but an increasing proportion of them give up work when they reach retirement age. In 1911, the proportion of men aged sixty-five and over at work was 59 per cent while in 1961 it was only 25 per cent; the corresponding proportions for women aged sixty and over at work were 13 per cent and 10 per cent respectively.

Four general factors account for the reduction in the proportion of the elderly at work. It is important to understand the operation of these factors for their combined impact is likely to lead to further reductions in the proportion of the old at work in the future. The mechanization and automation of many of the work processes has meant that technical skills soon become outdated and though this affects all age groups of the working population it affects the older working class workers most. Industry finds it financially more rewarding to absorb displaced workers who are young than those who are old. Automation, however, has raised an even greater question mark regarding the employment of the elderly. Automation has meant vastly increased productivity so that with rising population 'the labor of the aged has become increasingly superfluous'[6] in affluent societies, in the opinion of one commentator. Automation has, in other words, created a problem of leisure. There is no full-time work for all people in automated societies and the question then becomes as to how leisure should be allocated among members of society. One method generally approved is to raise the school leaving age and expand provisions for higher education. There is a limit, however, to how far this can go for the further exclusion of the young from paid employment, even if sponsored by the State, creates problems regarding the relationship of the young in their late teens to the rest of society. Leisure may also be taken in the form of a reduction in the number of days or hours or both worked every week. Again there has been a trend towards shorter working hours but it has not gone far enough to ease the problem of unemployment. It may be difficult or economically unprofitable to reduce substantially the hours of the working week or to reduce the number of working days because it may mean shift work which requires a great deal more management organization and is generally unpopular. This is not to say that there is no room for reduction in the length of the working week because so far what reductions there have been made in the official hours of work have been nullified by overtime work. Generally the pointers are that to cope with the problems of leisure created by increased automation society may have to rely on retirement from work more than it did in the past. The present practices whereby employers retire their employees as soon as they reach retirement age, or of retiring prematurely older workers made redundant and paying them adequate compensation, are likely to spread even more in the future.

The second reason for the reduction in the numbers of elderly in the labour force is the improvement in the state and occupational pensions with the result that for some of the elderly the financial need to work no longer exists or at least is no longer as pressing as it was in the past. It is not only the willingness to work that is affected but also the 'ability' for, as Wedderburn has stated,[7] 'If the only alternative to being able to work is to starve, then a man may go on being "able" to work for much longer than if he feels he can choose to stop.' All the indications are that the standard of pensions *vis-à-vis* the incomes of people at work will be better in the future than it is today particularly when the expansion of private pension schemes is taken into account. It is true that there will be social class differences in this as there are today but it does not alter the fact that the elderly of the future will probably enjoy relatively higher standards of living than the elderly of today.

The structure of the State scheme of retirement pensions is another possible factor discouraging the elderly from working. The Beveridge recommendations that formed the basis of the legislation on post-war retirement pension schemes reflected the ambiguity that surrounded then, and still surrounds today, the retirement role. The Beveridge Report did not accept the thesis that at a certain age people should automatically give up their working role and assume their new role of retirement. Rather it hoped that as many people as possible would not give up their working role at the minimum retirement age and that they would continue fulfilling their working role for as long as possible after that. Those who decided to give up work and retire would receive a State retirement pension adequate for subsistence; those who decided to postpone retirement altogether would receive nothing from the State while they were at work but when they eventually retired would receive slightly higher pensions; and those who decided to combine work and retirement would lose part of their pension depending on the amount of the wages they earned. It was a formula designed to reduce the costs of pensions and to encourage people to stay on at work. It conceded the principle of retirement rather hesitantly and by the attempts it made to encourage people to stay at work the Beveridge Report indirectly re-asserted the view that people should maintain themselves as long as possible. It is difficult to follow the logic of how the immediate deductions and eventual additions to pensions would encourage employment beyond the minimum retirement age. By penalizing financially those who continued working the system discourages employment among the elderly; the inducement of higher pensions for those who continue work has never been effective because the extra pension amounts gained have never been large enough. In general then, one cannot but agree with Piachaud's verdict[8] that 'the existing arrangements must discourage many old men from continuing to work', though one does not have to agree with his other conclusion that 'it is regrettable that the social security system has this effect'. If the labour of the elderly is not essential to economic growth, as we argued above, then there is no reason why the State should encourage them to work. What the State should do is to provide them with an adequate income to enjoy the same standard of living as the rest of the population. The abolition of the twin schemes of the earnings rule and of the pension increments is justified not because they discourage old people from working but because they assert that people ought to work beyond retirement age if they want to enjoy a standard of living above subsistence.

The fourth and last factor which may help to explain the reduction in the labour force participation among the elderly is the increased acceptance of the emerging new role of retirement. The literature on this issue is contradictory reflecting the transformation which the retirement role is undergoing at present. On the one hand more and more old people are giving up employment as soon as possible. The International Labour Organization recognized this trend when it declared that people today 'do not want to wait until they are worn out and have one foot in the grave' before they retire from work; they hope for 'a final holiday with pay'.[9] On the other hand, several studies[10] have found that retirement is a traumatic experience, that people find it difficult to adjust to retirement and that many would rather be at work. The recent cross-national study of old people[11] brought out these conflicting findings when it concluded that:

> Positive as well as negative attitudes to retirement are common. Adjustment to retirement varies. Some people appreciate the rest and the opportunity to spend their time as they please. More than half of all retired men in the United States and Britain and half of all retired men in Denmark specify that they enjoy rest and other things in retirement. Others resent the loss not only of money but the

feeling of being useful, the respect of others, and the enjoyment of the work itself.

Generally the findings of these studies are indicative of the fact that public attitudes towards retirement are in a melting pot; they are in a transitional stage out of which eventually a clearer role of retirement will emerge. Society is beginning to accept the fact that at a certain age in life, a person is expected to give up work and he is entitled to receive an adequate pension from the State as of right without loss of dignity or self-esteem. The adjustment of an individual in society is influenced not only by his personal perception of his situation but also by the public's attitude towards his situation. A clearer, institutionalized role of retirement will enable people to accept naturally retirement from work and to adjust better to their new situation. With better pensions, better housing, better health, longer years in retirement, society can anticipate the development of a subculture of leisure for the old— 'a development which may, by making old age a more attractive period in life, raise the prestige of this age group'.[12] In the same way that a culture for the leisure of the young has emerged in the middle of the twentieth century, the signs are that a culture for the old may emerge by the end of the twentieth century.

The economic circumstances of the elderly

The economic insecurity of the elderly has been such a long-standing feature of British society that it has become part of the national cultural system. It is expected and accepted that the elderly will face financial stresses, crises and deprivations. The fundamental explanation for the economic insecurity of the elderly is to be found in the dominant economic values of society which dictate that the allocation of goods and services in society must be patterned on people's income from work or from private resources. If people have to rely on income from the State to pay for the goods and services they need or demand, then they should expect a drop in their economic ability to do this. Income from the State should not be as great as income from work. In this way the financial circumstances of the elderly are on the whole worse than the financial circumstances of people at work. The climax to this economic doctrine has been the growth of earnings-related benefits we referred to in chapter 1. The prevalent view now is that not only must people's incomes in retirement be generally lower than their incomes from work but also that a direct proportional relationship must exist between retirement pensions and income from work during working life. The economically weak of the wage structure will also be the economically weak of the retirement pension structure; vice versa, the affluent at work, with more personal savings and more private insurance coverage, will also get the highest pension from the State.

The economic circumstances of the elderly have been fairly well documented in the 1960s—certainly far better than the circumstances of other minority groups requiring the help of the social security services. This reflects the greater numbers of the elderly *vis-à-vis* the other groups and society's greater concern for the plight of the elderly than the plight of other minority groups. Ageing is, after all, a natural physiological process and unlike the condition of other minority groups it implies no direct or indirect personal fault, inadequacy or blame. We shall summarize here the main features of the findings of the various studies on the elderly leaving out the details which, though interesting, do not alter the central theme of our arguments.

First, a high proportion of the elderly live in subsistence poverty, i.e. their total incomes from all sources are less than the supplementary benefit level including rent. The government study in 1965[13] showed that 14 per cent of all retirement pensioners would have received national assistance had they applied for it, i.e. they were living below the official poverty line. This was a slightly higher figure than the 11 per cent estimated by Townsend and Wedderburn in their study of old people in 1962.[14] The difference between the two figures is understandable for the government study looked at old people who had retired from work while the other study examined the position of all old people including those at work whose financial position is better than that of the retired. The three reasons which old people gave for not applying for national assistance were that they did not know how to go about applying, a feeling that they could somehow manage and a dislike of applying because they considered national assistance with its means tests as a form of charity. These three reasons are inter-related for lack of understanding or misunderstanding of a service can be not only a barrier in itself to the use of the service but can also create an emotional barrier militating against the use of that service even after enough is known about the provisions of that service. Vice versa, a service which for one reason or another is considered by the public to be 'stigmatized' is likely to be both misunderstood and not adequately understood for the perceived 'stigma' tends to distort any information about the service that reaches the public. Prejudice and fear cannot always be modified or eliminated by information alone. The evidence of the government study showed how deeply embedded notions of 'stigma' and charity are in the national culture. The younger age groups of the elderly who did not apply for assistance were just as likely to give 'charity' or 'pride' as reasons for not applying as the older age groups of the elderly were. Social values, attitudes and beliefs do not change rapidly nor are they so different among adjoining age groups. The 'stigma' attached to the receipt of national assistance has lingered and affects the use of its successor—the supplementary benefit—and is likely to persist whatever name it is given so long as the conditions under which it is granted remain less favourable than the conditions relating to the payment of insurance benefits.

Second, the scheme of national assistance has not performed a residual role as was intended in 1948 but it has instead played a major role for retirement pensioners and other beneficiaries. The government survey in 1965 showed that 78 per cent of all retirement pensioners had total retirement pensions which were no more than 25p higher than the flat rate retirement pension—an indication of the relative unimportance of the scheme of increments in pensions and of the graduated retirement pension. Not all these 78 per cent would, of course, have qualified for supplementary benefit because the majority had incomes from other sources in addition to their retirement pension. Some of them received amounts which were large enough to disqualify them from supplementary benefit. The two main sources of other income were earnings from work and occupational pensions. Savings were relatively unimportant. Whether a pensioner worked or had an occupational pension made a great deal of difference to his standard of living. Thus the proportion of those retirement pensioners without an occupational pension who fell below the national assistance level was three times greater than the corresponding proportion of those with occupational pensions.

Even taking all the various sources of income into account and in addition to the retirement pension, 47 per cent of the retirement pensioners had incomes below the national assistance level. As we just saw not everyone who is entitled to supplementary benefit applies but many do. The proportion of retirement pensioners drawing supplementary benefit varies slightly from year to year and not only has it shown no decline over the years but a slight rise. It has averaged about a quarter of all retirement pensioners every year since 1948.

The main reason for this reliance of pensioners on supplementary benefit is the fact that the supplementary benefit includes an amount for rent while the retirement pension does not. This applies to the other insurance benefits though not to the same extent because of the fairly adequate earnings-related supplements now paid for the first six months. Somehow the State has come to regard housing as an uninsurable necessity and it does not, therefore, include an allowance specifically for rent in the insurance benefits. The two reasons which have been given for this by various government spokesmen from time to time are that such an allowance will be costly and that the amount of the allowance will be too large for some beneficiaries and not large enough for others because the amount of people's rent varies so considerably. It is difficult to see on what rational grounds these two arguments have been confined to housing only and they have not been extended to cover other necessities such as clothes or food. A logical extension of these two arguments would result in the abolition of all insurance benefits and their replacement by supplementary benefits. In its very nature, as Burns has said,[15] 'social insurance deals with *presumptive* rather than *demonstrated* need, and is a social institution dominated by a concept of *average* rather than *individual* need'.

Third, there is a strong social class bias in the financial resources of the elderly. This is shown in a variety of ways most of which reflect the hard realities of a stratified society. The higher social classes are more likely to be receiving occupational pensions and also to be receiving larger amounts than the working classes. Thus the government survey showed that three in ten of retirement pensioners who prior to retirement were manual workers received an occupational pension; the corresponding proportion for the formerly non-manual workers was six in ten. The average occupational pension received by retirement pensioners with a non-manual background was three times greater than that received by those with a manual background. A similar picture applies to savings, personal insurance policies and earnings from work. Above all there is a cumulative effect with the result that the retired with total high incomes have incomes from various sources. Those with high incomes are more likely to be those with a non-manual occupation though other factors such as age and sex can distort this picture. The cross-national study found the median total money income 'of the blue collar group is 68 per cent of that of the white collar group'.[16] The flat rate retirement pension scheme discriminates against those whose working lives had been subjected to long and frequent interruptions since the award of the pension and its amount is related, albeit vaguely, to the pensioner's insurance contribution record.

Fourth, there are substantial income inequalities among the aged according to such demographic factors as age, sex and marital status. The very old are less likely to have occupational pensions and to have occupational pensions of lower value due partly to inflation; they are less likely to be in employment and more likely to have used up their savings. Thus the government study[17] in 1965 showed that while only one in five of all retirement pensioners relied exclusively on their retirement pension and the supplementary benefit allowance, the corresponding proportion among those aged eighty-five years and over was almost one in two. The cross-national study[18] confirmed this by showing that the median total money income dropped with advancing age. It is in recognition of these facts that an age supplement to the retirement pension was introduced in 1971—25p a week is added to the pension for people aged eighty or over. This addition, though welcome, is far too small to compensate for the deprivation of this age group and does not alter significantly their condition. That the financial position of retired women who are single or widowed is worse than that of men is to be expected. It follows naturally from their inferior position in the economic and occupational structure during working life. They are less likely to be in regular employment, more likely to earn low wages and less likely to be covered by an occupational pension. The fact, too, that they live longer than men exacerbates their situation further. The very old widows are, perhaps, the most vulnerable group among the elderly. The retirement pension with its emphasis on insurance and retirement from work is both meaningless and discriminatory against this population group for most of them were never in regular employment for long. They rely largely on incomes for which their deceased husband qualified, some of which lapse with his death, and others dwindle by the time they reach advanced old age. In a male-dominated world, pensions are based on the work histories of men—their earnings, insurance record and retirement age—yet most old people in retirement are women, particularly the very old and the very poor.

Proposals for reform

Social security is a political issue because it affects the interests both of the poor as well as the rich. It is an area where the 'end of ideology' thesis can be tested and since retirement pensions make up about 60 per cent of the total expenditure on social security we shall use the proposals of the two major parties for pension reform as our example. We shall do this by analysing the proposals which the two governments in their respective White Papers[19] made with regard to the standard, the finance, the coverage and the administration of pensions.

The Labour government proposals envisaged the payment of the full earnings-related pension after contributions had been paid for twenty years. The amount of the pension would be calculated on the person's previous earnings according to the following formula: 60 per cent of the retired person's earnings up to half the national average earnings of industrial workers; and 25 per cent of the remainder of his earnings up to one and a half times the national average earnings which is the scheme's ceiling. Those too old to pay contributions for the full twenty-year period would earn parts of the pension depending on the number of years they had contributed to the scheme. Once paid, retirement pensions would be reviewed every two years to compensate for at least the rise in prices. The retired person's previous earnings for each year of his working life are expressed as a percentage of the national average earnings; these annual percentages are averaged and it is on the final average percentage that the person's retirement pension is based. This method ensures that a person's whole earnings history is taken into account, both his good and bad years. The scheme attempted to help those with weak work histories by crediting them with contributions during periods of unemployment and sickness.[20]

The Conservative proposals envisage the payment of two pensions to each employee—the basic flat rate pension and either an occupational pension or a government earnings-related pension. The government's intention is to encourage employers to provide occupational pensions and only those employees not covered by occupational pensions will come under the State reserve scheme for earnings-related pensions. To gain recognition and thus exemption from the State reserve scheme, an occupational pension scheme must satisfy certain standards, which are generally recognized as being very low because they are intended to encourage the growth of occupational pensions. The government acknowledged the inadequacy of many of the existing occupational pension schemes and it proposed the setting up of the Occupational Pensions Board to encourage improvements and expansion of occupational pension schemes. Flat rate retirement pensions are to be reviewed annually to take account at least of the rise in prices but both the government earnings-related pension and the occupational pensions are static, i.e. the amount of pension paid on retirement is not increased thereafter to take account of either the rise in prices or wages. This is a serious drawback bearing in mind the high rate of inflation and the rise in standards of living in advanced industrial societies.

Comparisons between the level of pensions in the schemes of the two governments is impossible because of the reliance of the Conservative scheme on occupational pensions. There is no doubt, however, that the Labour government scheme *guaranteed* a higher pension to the average wage-earner than the scheme of the Conservative government did. It may well be that employers will provide occupational pensions far in excess of the stipulated minimum. It may well also be true that the position of those relying completely on the Conservative State scheme may have to be improved in the future because of the political pressure that the seven million pensioners involved may exert. As Heclo said,[21] it is difficult to believe 'that this large group and their spokesmen will, in the years ahead, settle for fifth-rate pensions and stagnant benefits'. But these are speculations to be proved rather than to be taken for granted.

The similarities between the two schemes exceed their dissimilarities. They both accept that the State either through its own schemes or those of the employers should encourage the persistence and in some ways the growth of income inequality during retirement. This agreement on fundamentals clearly limits differences between the two party schemes to matters of detail and administration. Thus under both schemes, income inequalities during retirement will continue to be widespread as they are today. The higher a person's income during working life, the higher his retirement pension will be. Since wages continually rise, there will also be inequalities based on age with the younger retired receiving pensions which are higher than those of the older retired. There will also be inequalities according to sex because women's contributions earn lower retirement pensions than those of men. Women retire earlier and live longer than men and though both events are largely beyond their control they are still to be penalized. The self-employed of average and low income will receive lower pensions than employees of the same economic standing because both government schemes make less generous provisions for them. In future then income inequalities will continue to exist between the retired and the working population as well as among the various groups of the retired simply because the public, the political parties and the country's leaders cannot divest themselves of their traditional beliefs, values and prejudices. The *status quo* continues, benefiting the rich and the powerful as it has always done.

The financial arrangements for both schemes are very similar. They both rely on earnings-related contributions. Perhaps the main innovation is the proposal that the flat rate retirement pension in the Conservative scheme is to be financed out of earnings-related contributions of employees, employers and a subsidy from the State. This is a departure from the past and it is more favourable to vertical redistribution of income bearing in mind, however, that income above one and a half times the national average is disregarded. But if the Conservative finance proposals are more progressive than the Labour scheme proposals in one respect, they are less so in another. The State earnings-related scheme is to be financed out of contributions from employers and employees and unlike the Labour government's earnings-related scheme involves no subsidy from the Exchequer. This means that a person's pension is determined exclusively by his contributions and those of his employers with no attempt from the government to help the low-paid workers. In general, then, the two political parties are agreed on the methods of financing retirement pensions: they have both rejected the idea of financing pensions largely out of government funds like education or health; they have both kept their faith in the insurance principle; and they have both moved away from flat rate to earnings-related contributions.

Both schemes are comprehensive in their coverage. They both envisage that employees are compulsorily insured though they differ on the methods they propose to achieve this. The Conservative scheme, however, loses some of its comprehensiveness by the mere fact that it relies on occupational pensions. Many employees lose or cash their pension rights when they change employers. The Conservative scheme attempts to improve this situation by encouraging, but not compelling, occupational pension schemes to introduce transfer arrangements wherever possible so that employees who change jobs maintain their pension rights throughout their years of employment. Where transfer arrangements are not possible, all workers over the age of twenty-six with five years' pensionable service who leave their jobs are paid a deferred pension by their ex-employer when they eventually retire. Clearly this will involve a great deal of administrative complexity bearing also in mind that the pensions provided by different employers will vary in generosity and also that many employees will not only move from one occupational pension to another but also in and out of the government reserve scheme.

The great divide between the schemes of the two governments is on the relative importance of State and occupational pensions. The Conservative government accepts full responsibility for the flat rate retirement pension but hopes that occupational pensions will be largely run by employers. It is estimated that its reserve scheme will cover only seven million employees or about one-quarter of the labour force consisting mainly of low-paid workers. The better paid will be catered for by the occupational pensions provided by the employers themselves with the aid of the private insurance societies. The Labour government accepted full responsibility for the retirement pensions of everyone but conceded the principle that employers had a right to contract their employees out of the State scheme provided they satisfied certain minimum requirements. It is not possible to know in advance what proportion of employees would have been contracted out of the State scheme but it is generally agreed that it would not have reached the same proportion as that of the Conservative scheme. Though the two schemes are based on opposing philosophies on this issue, in practice they work towards convergence because their philosophies are flexible enough to accommodate the demands of the market. Once the Labour government permitted contracting out, it offered those contracted out certain advantages over those left in the State scheme; contributions to occupational pensions enjoy income tax relief while this does not apply for contributions to the State scheme: occupational pension schemes are not subject to the earnings rule but the State earnings-related scheme would have been on similar lines to the present flat rate retirement pension; people in non-contributory occupational pensions do not pay any contributions; and finally, the retirement age in some occupational pension schemes is lower than that in the State scheme. Contracting-out also offered the very real advantage to the large employer of allowing him to use the contributions of his employees and of the firm for investment purposes. Clearly contracting-out had important economic implications for the employers, the employees and the private insurance societies.

In general, the Conservative and Labour pension schemes are very similar in their essential characteristics though they naturally differ in many details. They both envisage that the financial circumstances of the elderly should be unequal ranging from those, few though they may be, whose retirement pension will be lower than the supplementary benefit amount to those, few again though they may be, whose combined State, occupational and private pension could amount to more than the high salaries they were earning while at work. Though both schemes will transfer more income to the elderly as a group, poverty will still exist among more or less the same groups of the elderly who are today in poverty.

6

∽∾∽∾∽∾∽∾∽∾∽∾∽

Social security
and society

∽∾∽∾∽∾∽∾∽∾∽∾∽

In this final chapter we bring together mainly ideas expressed in previous chapters of the social, economic and political functions of social security. We attempt to do this by examining the intended and unintended inter-relationships between social security on one hand and the family, social class and work on the other.

The family

In the absence of an explicit government family policy, the inter-relationship between social security and the family is likely to be haphazard, contradictory and at times negative. Social security often walks the tightrope between its wishes to support the family and its fear lest the help it provides undermines either the very family virtues it wants to foster or other social values that override family considerations.

The most positive way in which social security supports the family is also the most obvious—the payment of allowances not only for the insured person himself but also for his wife and children. This has not always been the case for under the National Insurance Act, 1911, the sickness and unemployment benefit paid to the insured person did not include any allowances for his dependants. The extension of social security benefits to cover the needs of the whole family was both logical and inevitable. It reflected society's greater stress on the social service aspects of social security as distinct from its actuarial and narrowly defined economic aspects.

The introduction of earnings-related benefits in the 1960s with no allowances for dependants and with a wages stop ruling is a regressive step in the sense that it emphasizes vague and dubious economic criteria at the expense of family considerations. A basic aim of a social service is to promote equality and reduce inequality and earnings-related benefits are a denial of this however subtly justified.[1]

Though parents are legally and otherwise held responsbile for the well-being of each of their children, the State, too, has a strong vested interest in the stability of the family and the welfare of the children. As mentioned earlier, in an industrial society the children are the nation's most precious asset and for purely economic, if for no other, reasons their education and general welfare is of paramount concern to the State. Added to this is the fact which Wynn so forcibly made that the burden of rearing the next generation at any one time falls on only a small minority of the households in the country.[2] These two vital facts receive faint government recognition by the payment of family allowances, family income supplements and attendance allowances for disabled members of the family. The amounts of these allowances and the conditions under which they are paid reflect the contradictory value system that sustains them. The main fears are that if the amount of family allowances was adequate for the full maintenance of children it might undermine parental responsibility; and that if the amount of family income supplement closed the whole gap between low family wages and the official poverty line it might harm work incentives. All these and other fears as well as considerations about the added economic costs involved have meant that government financial aid to the family has so far been negligible and minimum. Nevertheless it represents a cautious step away from the doctrines of the economic man and of rigid filial responsibility.

The doctrine of filial responsibility is a natural and a necessary outcome of the central role of the family in social organization. For a variety of demographic, social, economic and political factors, the family circle within which filial responsibility legally operates has been narrowed and the conditions for its legal enforcement have been liberalized over the years. The harsh enforcement of the doctrine of filial responsibility within the wide extended family circle meant that the poor supported the poor and in doing so they made it that much more difficult for themselves to rise above poverty.[3] The same applies today but to a much smaller extent for filial responsibility is not so absolute and it does not extend beyond the nuclear family circle.

Necessary though the limited concept of filial responsibility is, its enforcement still has unintended harmful effects on the functioning of the family. Thus unemployed fathers who draw supplementary benefit and who are considered to be persistently refusing work can be prosecuted and sent to prison.[4] Not only can filial responsibility lead to the break-up of families, it can also make reunification more difficult. Thus deserting fathers whose families draw supplementary benefit must be prosecuted for maintenance and those who do not comply with the conditions of the maintenance order can again be sentenced to imprisonment. Finally, filial responsibility can make the re-establishment of two-parent family units difficult. Separated or divorced wives who are in receipt of supplementary benefit will lose that benefit if they remarry or cohabit. While this follows naturally from society's central value that parents must support each other and their children, is society justified in expecting the new husband to take over total responsibility particularly in the case of large families ?

The doctrine of filial responsibility has also led social security to the paradoxical situation where it is financially better for the family that the father should die rather than leave the family or be disabled and continue living with the family. Thus while widowed mothers will receive an insurance benefit for themselves and their children irrespective of any other income which they may have from work or elsewhere, separated or divorced mothers can only apply for supplementary benefit which is paid after a means test and which ceases if they take up full employment. Suggestions made by Beveridge and others after him for the provision of an insurance benefit for all one-parent families have foundered on the rock of matrimony. The value which society places on marriage militates against equality of treatment for all one-parent families. Separated and divorced families, unlike widowed families, are generally held partly responsible for their condition in addition to the fact that their conduct is seen as threatening to the institutions of marriage and family.[5]

Finally, social security has been linked in a variety of ways with fertility rates and the size of the family. The introduction of family allowances in many European countries was partly due to the belief that it might help to stem the decline in birth rates and perhaps even reverse that trend.[6] The experience of industrial countries has since been that fertility rates depend on a complex network of economic, cultural and demographic factors and the payment of a small weekly allowance per child makes little or no difference to the decision of a couple whether to have a child or not.[7] In spite of this evidence, the belief still persists that family allowances produce large families and since today we suffer from fears of over-population rather than under-population as was the case in the 1930s when the public debate on the introduction of family allowances was taking place, this belief is one of the reasons for the lack of government urgency to improve family allowances.

In brief, then, while society supports the stability of the family and the welfare of children, it also supports other values related to work, self-support and individualism with the result that social security provision for the family is half-hearted, conditional and at times even negative.

Social class

Social security involves the collection and payment of vast sums of money every year and can, therefore, have important effects on the distribution of income and possibly on the stratification system of the country. It is clear that social security involves a great deal of horizontal redistribution of income, i.e. from the employed to the unemployed, the healthy to the sick, from those without children to those with children, and so on. Social security also involves a great deal of income redistribution from one generation to another since retirement pensions are financed largely by the working population in direct and indirect ways. This type of income redistribution follows naturally from the basic principle of social insurance, i.e. the pooling of risks principle. What we are concerned with here, however, is whether social security involves any vertical redistribution of income, i.e. whether it reduces the extent of inequality between the classes.

It is not possible with the available evidence to be precise about vertical redistribution.[8] All that we can attempt is to paint a broad picture of the likely ways in which one social class pays more than another and benefits less than another from the social security services. The tripartite system of flat rate insurance contributions means that all members of the working force contribute more or less equally towards the finance of social security. Working-class employees may contribute less in the sense that they suffer more from unemployment, sickness and disability during which periods no contributions are paid. On the other hand, middle- and upper-class employees pay less by the mere fact that since they stay on at school much longer than working-class people they start paying contributions later in life. It should also be borne in mind that flat rate contributions are a regressive form of taxation because they weigh more heavily on the lower-paid than on the better-paid. Earnings-related contributions, which could have been vertically redistributive, do not take into account income above one-and-a-half times the national average and they provide earnings-related benefits anyhow.

Employers' contributions involve no vertical redistribution of income since they do not lead to a reduction in profits. Their cost is passed on to the public in the form of higher prices or in lower wage rises.[9] Apart from employers' and employees' contributions to social security funds there is also the smaller proportion that comes from government funds. This contribution by the government may involve some vertical redistribution of income since government revenue is made up almost equally from direct taxes which are a progressive form of taxation and indirect taxes which 'are more likely to be regressive or at least roughly proportional'.[10] Any redistribution of income from the rich to the poor is contained in the very small proportion, about 10 per cent, of the social security revenue that comes from direct taxes through the government contribution. The methods used to finance social security are, on the whole, regressive and they involve no important elements of redistributing income from the rich to the poor.

It can, of course, be argued that though the vast majority of people contribute to the funds of social security equally, working-class persons are more likely to receive social security benefits than upper-class persons. This is true for those benefits which can be classed as being for forms of 'diswelfare', to use Titmuss's term,[11] i.e. a form of monetary compensation for the hardship they suffer through the operation of the social and economic system—benefits for industrial disability, unemployment and illness as well as supplementary benefit. It is not, however, true of retirement pensions and they after all account for at least half the expenditure of social security widely defined. Since retirement pensions are paid to all who have paid the necessary number of contributions they involve a negative form of vertical redistribution of income—from the poor to the rich—because retired persons of higher income groups live longer than those of lower income groups. This is of crucial importance because all the studies so far have examined the question of the redistributive effects of social security from a limited income period—at most during a period of twelve months.[12] It is not surprising therefore that they reached the conclusion that social security benefits the poor at the expense of the rich. Had they examined the question over a much longer period, preferably over the whole life cycle, they would have reached a different conclusion.[13] If one also takes into account the fact that occupational benefits for retirement, widowhood and sickness strongly favour the middle and upper classes, then the combined operation of the State and occupational benefits over the entire life cycle involves a negative form of vertical redistribution of income.

This general conclusion is not surprising since the Beveridge Report and the general thinking behind social security so far has not envisaged social security as a mechanism for the reduction of inequality in society. The function most commonly attributed to the social security system is the abolition of subsistence poverty. As we saw in previous chapters, social security has contributed a great deal in this direction but has failed to abolish subsistence poverty altogether. What we need to stress here is that as presently constituted, social security will not be much more successful in the future. Subsistence poverty exists in society because of three main features of the social security services: the first is the unwillingness to ensure that all those at work receive through wages and social security benefits an income equal at least to what they would have received in supplementary benefit. Second, poverty is condoned through the application of the wages stop and the various rulings regarding the 'voluntary unemployed'. Third, there is the reluctance of people to apply for supplementary benefit when they are not entitled to an insurance benefit, when their insurance benefit has run out or when it is not paid to them in full due to inadequate contribution records. This is made worse by the additional fact that the supplementary benefit is larger in amount than most flat rate insurance benefits for it can include an allowance for rent. The recent changes in social security—family income supplement and the new proposals for retirement pensions—reduce the effects of these three features of social security but they do not do away with them.

If the abolition of subsistence poverty is the best known of the functions of the social security service, the entrenchment of the position of the dominant classes is the least known of its functions. We discussed at length in previous chapters the ways in which the development of social security has always taken account of the dominant social values and the economic interests of the upper classes. We need only a brief addendum here but an important one. Though it is true that social security has helped to reduce the glaring injustices of capitalist industrialization and in this way undermined the will of the working classes for rapid and radical political changes, it is not correct to deduce from this that social security along with other social legislation has irretrievably blocked the path towards a socialist-egalitarian society. The achievements of the Welfare State have been slow, gradual and below initial expectations. They have also benefited the middle and upper classes as much as the working classes, if not more. This, coupled with the fact that they have been arrived at in a predominantly non-violent way, should neither detract from their contribution to the betterment of life nor from their potentiality for the future. Social reforms together with economic advancement have improved the position of the working class enough to enable it to feel secure and to aspire to middle- and upper-class standards of living. They may have, therefore, increased working-class feelings of relative deprivation—a situation which is potentially favourable to social change. It is in this respect that it can be argued that social reforms may have helped to increase demands for further improvements and changes in the social and economic system.

That such demands will be resisted by the dominant classes, as they have been resisted in the past, follows from the conflict model of society we have adopted in this book. That they will continue to succeed, however, in a gradual, compromising way, as they have done in the past, is more than likely.

Work

The value which society places on work has traditionally been closely associated with the value of individualism and as a result it has had negative effects on the development of social security. It has meant that in the first place the amount of benefits must be small lest people's willingness to work and support themselves suffers. Even today with flat rate and earnings-related benefits, the total amount of the benefit must always be smaller than the person's wages for fear of malingering. 'The purpose of social security,' said Huntford referring to Sweden's comparatively generous benefits,[14] 'is to dispel need without crossing the threshold of prosperity.' Second, social security benefits are granted under conditions designed to reduce the likelihood of even the boldest of spirits attempting to live on the State rather than work. Many of the rules surrounding the payment of unemployment or supplementary benefit are for this purpose. Third, the value placed on work is manifested in a more positive way as in the case of disability. People suffering from accidents incurred at work or from occupational diseases receive preferential treatment by the social security service compared with those suffering from civil accidents and ordinary illnesses.[15]

Yet, as we saw earlier in this chapter, the stranglehold which work has had on the social security service has been increasingly loosened over the years. The provision of family allowances, family income supplements, the slight liberalization of the wages stop are some of the manifestations of this trend. Similarly, the preferential treatment given to occupational disability by the social security service has been increasingly questioned with the demands for the upgrading of benefits for the other types of disability. It is felt that in contemporary industrial societies the distinction between occupational and non-occupational disability is artificial for many non-occupational forms of disability have an industrial origin even if they do not occur directly in the workplace.[16] There is also the additional reason which we mentioned in the argument for one benefit for all one-parent families, that a modern social security service must concentrate on meeting needs irrespective of the causes behind such needs.

The relationship between social security and work is not all a one-way affair. It is true that until very recently the general view was that social security 'represented a type of luxury and was essentially anti-economic'.[17] It was seen as merely government expenditure for the needy. As we saw, however, in chapter 4, redundancy payments and earnings-related unemployment benefits have been used with some success by employers and the government to reduce workers' opposition towards loss of their jobs with all that this means in terms of production, profits, etc.

Social security has also important implications for such economic activities as saving, investment and consumption even though there is no adequate understanding of these inter-relationships among economists. Insurance contributions are a form of saving which in funded insurance schemes can be an important source of investment for industrial expansion and profit making. The preference for occupational pensions in the Conservative scheme for retirement pensions was motivated by these economic considerations even if it was presented to the public in the glossy image of individualism and self-support. There is also better awareness today that social security benefits can be important to industrial production and the level of employment by their effect on the consumption of goods and services in the market. Social security benefits enable the non-working sections of the population to become purchasing groups and this can be particularly useful in stimulating demand at times of temporary industrial stagnation.

Rimlinger's statement[18] that 'The institution of social security programs can be no more neutral in the economic than it is in the social sense' has been one of the major themes of our discussion. Its past development has been along ideological lines and its future growth will inevitably be linked closely with ideology. There are no objective, scientific criteria which can tell us how to choose between the various alternatives. We have to rely on our values and beliefs much more than on facts. The social scientist has an important part to play not merely as a fact gatherer and as a social engineer but, more important, as a radical critic of society and as an advocate of 'Utopian' changes to the existing social and economic system. As Marcuse has said,[19] 'it is the task and duty of the intellectual to recall and preserve historical possibilities which seem to have become utopian possibilities . . . it is his task to break the concreteness of oppression in order to open the mental space in which this society can be recognized as what it is and does.' Such a role is both constructive and promising for the future for in the words of Weber,[20] 'all political experience confirms the truth—that man would not have achieved the possible unless time and again he had reached out for the impossible.'

Conclusion

The radical social security service that this book proposes must satisfy the following five criteria. First, it should aim at achieving a substantial reduction in income inequality in society. This would mean that the social security service should be financed out of taxation and that it should provide adequate flat rate benefits without reference to insurance contribution records and without the imposition of the wages stop ruling. Second, it should seek to reduce stratified social relationships. The beneficiaries of the service should be encouraged to participate in a meaningful way in the administration of the various related departments and agencies on a national and local level. Third, it should encourage respect for and acceptance of people making use of the service. This would require professional training for the administrators as well as the provision of office facilities that make the implementation of such a policy possible. It would also mean that the institutional conditions for the payment of benefits should be non-stigmatizing and non-discriminatory. Fourth, the legal and administrative conditions should aim at encouraging equality of access to the service by all sections of the community. Rules about entitlement to benefits should not be departmental secrets; legal aid should be granted to those wishing to challenge decisions of the administrators; and so on. Finally, the social security service should not be an inferior partner to market provision. Occupational benefits in their present form should either be made subordinate to the social service criteria mentioned above or preferably they should be abolished. Similarly, private insurance pension schemes should be discouraged by the abolition of the existing relevant income tax concessions that benefit the wealthier section of the community most. Only when every citizen, irrespective of income, occupation and sex, is helped solely or mainly by the social security service when his income from work ceases or is interrupted will the social security benefits be fixed at a high enough level to provide a decent standard of living. Based on these five principles, the social security service can help to reduce the inequalities of income, status and power prevalent in contemporary British society as well as fulfil adequately its traditional role of income maintenance.

∞∞∞∞∞

Notes

∞∞∞∞∞

1 The development of social security and the ruling classes

1 Timms, N., *A Sociological Approach to Social Problems*, Routledge & Kegan Paul, 1967, Ch. 1.
2 Rex, J., *Key Problems in Sociological Theory*, Routledge & Kegan Paul, 1961, pp. 129–31, for a summary of the conflict model of the social system used in this discussion.
3 Atkinson, D., *Orthodox Consensus and Radical Alternative*, Heinemann, 1971, p. 250.
4 For a concise discussion of theories of social order, see Cohen, P. S., *Modern Social Theory*, Heinemann, 1968, Ch. 2.
5 Coser, L., 'The sociology of poverty', *Social Problems*, vol. 13, 1965.
6 Jordan, W. K., *Philanthropy in England, 1480–1660*, Allen & Unwin, 1959, p. 55.
7 Ibid., pp. 55–6.
8 Ibid., p. 80.
9 Ibid., p. 77.
10 Rimlinger, G. V., *Welfare Policy and Industrialization in Europe, America and Russia*, Wiley, 1971, p. 19.
11 Tawney, R. H., *Religion and the Rise of Capitalism*, Penguin, 1948, p. 268, where Young's quotation is also to be found.
12 Ibid., p. 265.
13 Gray, B. Kirkman, *A History of English Philanthropy*, King, 1905, p. 32.
14 Schweinitz, K. de, *England's Road to Social Security*, University of Pennsylavania Press, 1961 ed., p. 119.
15 Ibid., p. 70.
16 Webb, S. and B., *English Poor Law History*, Longmans, Green, 1927, vol. I, p. 190.
17 Thompson, E. P., *The Making of the English Working Class*, Penguin, 1968, p. 244.
18 Bendix, R., *Work and Authority in Industry*, Wiley, 1956, p. 42.
19 Tawney, R. H., *Equality*, Allen & Unwin, 1964, p. 98.
20 Schweinitz, K. de, op. cit., p. 187.
21 *Report of the Royal Commission on the Poor Laws*, 1834, p. 228.
22 Quoted by Schweinitz, K. de, op. cit., p. 124.
23 McGregor, O. R., 'Social research and social policy in the nineteenth century', *British Journal of Sociology*, vol. 8, No. 1, March 1957.

24 Bendix, R., op. cit., p. 99.
25 Gilbert, B., *British Social Policy, 1914-1939*, Batsford, 1970, p. 51.
26 Rimlinger, G., 'Social Security and Industrialization' in Kassalow, E. (ed.), *The Role of Social Security in Economic Development*, U.S. Department of Health, Education and Welfare, 1968, p. 144.
27 Gilbert, B., *The Evolution of National Insurance in Great Britain*, Michael Joseph, 1966, p. 24.
28 Webb, B., *My Apprenticeship*, Longmans, Green, 1926, p. 174.
29 Rimlinger, G. V., *Welfare Policy and Industrialization in Europe, America and Russia*, Wiley, 1971, p. 337.
30 Gilbert, B., op. cit., p. 56.
31 Bendix, R., op. cit., p. 115.
32 Gilbert, B., op. cit., p. 448.
33 Rhys, V., 'The sociology of social security', *Bulletin of the International Social Security Association*, Nos. 1-2, 1962.
34 Marwick, A., 'The Labour Party and the Welfare State in Britain, 1900-1948', *American Historical Review*, 73, 1967. Rhys, V., in 'The sociology of social security', states that the Social Democratic Party of Germany was against the insurance principle when first introduced.
35 Rimlinger, G. V., *Welfare Policy and Industrialization in Europe, America and Russia*, p. 338.
36 *Labour's Call to the People*, Labour Manifesto, 1922, quoted in Craig, F. W. S. (ed.), *British General Election Manifestos, 1918-1966*, Political Reference Publications, 1970, p. 15.
37 Miliband, R., *Parliamentary Socialism*, Allen & Unwin, 1961, p. 148.
38 Tawney, R. H., *Equality*, pp. 205-6.
39 Cripps, S., *Can Socialism Come by Constitutional Means ?*, London (n.d.), p. 2.
40 Tawney, R. H., *Equality*, p. 202.
41 Galbraith, J., *The New Industrial State*, Penguin, 1967, p. 32.
42 Inter-departmental Committee (Beveridge Report), *Social Insurance and Allied Services*, Cmd. 6404, HMSO, 1942.
43 Marwick, A., op. cit.
44 Miliband, R., op. cit., p. 307.
45 Government Actuary, *Occupational Pension Schemes*, HMSO, First Survey, 1956; Second Survey, 1966; Third Survey, 1968.
46 Titmuss, R. M., *Essays on the Welfare State*, Allen & Unwin, 1963 ed., p. 55.
47 Lynes, T., 'Social security research', in Young, M. (ed.), *Forecasting in the Social Sciences*, Heinemann, 1968, p. 140.
48 Rimlinger, G. V., *Welfare Policy and Industrialization in Europe, America and Russia*, p.343.
49 Butler, D. and Rose, R., *The British General Election of 1959*, Macmillan, 1960, p. 70.

50 Bell, D., *The End of Ideology*, Free Press, 1960, p. 405.
51 Ibid.
52 Marcuse, H., *One-Dimensional Man*, Sphere Books, 1968, p. 19.
53 Ibid., p. 200.
54 Horowitz, D., 'One-dimensional society', *International Socialist Journal*, Year 4, No. 24, December 1967.
55 Ibid.
56 Miliband, R., *The State in Capitalist Society*, Weidenfeld & Nicolson, 1969, p. 264.
57 Beveridge Report, para. 369.
58 Coser, L., op. cit.
59 Pinker, R., *Social Theory and Social Policy*, Heinemann, 1971, p. 142.
60 Central Statistical Office, *Social Trends*, No. 2, HMSO, 1971, Table 44, p. 90.

2 Poverty and the social security system today

1 Galbraith, J., *The Affluent Society*, Penguin, 1962, p. 262.
2 Ibid., p. 263.
3 Ibid., p. 263.
4 Lewis, O., *The Children of Sanchez*, Secker & Warburg, 1962, p. 24.
5 Gans, H., *People and Plans*, Penguin, 1972, p. 309.
6 Marsden, D., review of *Culture and Poverty: critique and counter-proposals*, by C. A. Valentine, Chicago University Press, 1968, in *Poverty*, No. 11, Summer, 1969.
7 Smith, A., *The Wealth of Nations*, Book 5, Ch. 2, Part 2.
8 Quoted in Meissner, H. (ed.), *Poverty in the Affluent Society*, Harper & Row, 1966, p. 203.
9 Rein, M., in Townsend, P. (ed.), *The Concept of Poverty*, Heinemann, 1970, p. 46.
10 Coates, K. and Silburn, R., *Poverty: The Forgotten Englishmen*, Penguin, 1970, p. 26.
11 Meade, J., *Efficiency, Equality and the Ownership of Property*, Allen & Unwin, 1964, p. 39.
12 Rowntree, B. S., *Poverty: A Study of Town Life*, Macmillan, 1901; Rowntree, B. S., *Poverty and Progress: A Second Social Survey of York*, Longmans, 1941.
13 Rowntree, B. S., *Poverty: A Study of Town Life*, p.87.
14 Ibid., pp. 133-4.
15 Orshansky, M., 'Counting the poor: another look at the poverty profile', *Social Security Bulletin*, 28, No. 1, January 1965.
16 Rowntree, B. S., *Poverty: A Study of Town Life*, p. 99.
17 Ibid., p. 137.
18 Ibid., pp. 107-8.

19 Ibid., p. 106.
20 These percentages are based on Rowntree's statement that, 'In 1899 the average wage of the male heads of families was 27s. 5d. In 1936 it was 63s. 0d.' (Rowntree, B. S., *Poverty and Progress*, p. 452.) Since his poverty line for 1899 and 1936 for a family of five was 21s. 8d. and 53s. 0d. respectively, the percentages are as given here and not 79 per cent for 1899 and 69 per cent for 1936 as stated by Abel-Smith, B., and Townsend, P., in *The Poor and the Poorest*, Bell, 1965, p. 16. What Abel-Smith and Townsend did was to use the poverty line of 1899 inclusive of rent but to use the poverty line of 1936 exclusive of rent.
21 Beveridge Report, p. 77.
22 Burnett, J., *A History of the Cost of Living Index*, Penguin, 1969, p. 307.
23 Roach, J. and Roach, J. (eds), *Poverty*, Penguin, 1972, p. 16.
24 Lynes, T., *National Assistance and National Prosperity*, Codicote, 1962. See also Department of Employment *Gazette*, June 1969.
25 Townsend, P., 'The meaning of poverty', *British Journal of Sociology*, vol. 13, 1962.
26 Zöllner, D., 'Relating social insurance benefits to earnings', *International Social Security Review*, vol. 23, No. 2, 1970.
27 Rowntree, B. S. and Lavers, G. R., *Poverty and the Welfare State*, Longmans, 1951.
28 Ministry of Labour and National Service, *Report of an Enquiry into Household Expenditure in 1953–4*, HMSO, 1957.
29 Townsend, P., *The Family Life of Old People*, Routledge & Kegan Paul, 1957.
30 Cole, D. and Utting, J., *The Economic Circumstances of Old People*, Codicote, 1962.
31 Marris, P., *Widows and Their Families*, Routledge & Kegan Paul, 1958.
32 Abel-Smith, B. and Townsend, P., *The Poor and the Poorest*, Bell, 1965.
33 Ministry of Pensions and National Insurance, *Financial and Other Circumstances of Retirement Pensioners*, HMSO, 1966.
34 Ministry of Social Security, *Circumstances of Families*, HMSO, 1967.
35 Rowntree, B. S., *Poverty: A Study of Town Life*, pp. 136–7.
36 Seligman, B. (ed.), *Poverty as a Public Issue*, Free Press, 1965, p. 1.
37 Tawney, R., 'Poverty as an industrial problem', Inaugural Lecture of the Ratan Tata Foundation, 1913, p. 9., quoted in Rose, M., *The Relief of Poverty 1834–1914*, Macmillan, 1972, p. 52.
38 Townsend, P., *Poverty, Socialism and Labour in Power*, Fabian Tract 371, Fabian Society, 1967, p. 31.
39 Saville, J., 'Labourism and the Labour Government', *Socialist Register*, Merlin Press, 1967, p. 69.

3 Low pay and social security

1 Atkinson, A., *Poverty in Britain and the Reform of Social Security*, Cambridge University Press, 1969, Table 5.1, p. 81.
2 National Board for Prices and Incomes, *General Problems of Low Pay*, HMSO, Cmnd. 4648, 1971, p. 6.
3 Ibid., p. 9.
4 Wootton, B., *The Social Foundations of Wage Policy*, Allen & Unwin, 1962 ed., p. 163.
5 Sheridan, G., 'Women, cheap labour', *Guardian*, 4 February 1972.
6 National Board for Prices and Incomes, *Productivity, Prices and Incomes Policy after 1969*', Cmnd. 4237, HMSO, December 1969, para. 61.
7 Department of Employment and Productivity, *A National Minimum Wage*, HMSO, 1969, p. 3.
8 Ibid., p. 5.
9 Hughes, J., in Bull, D. (ed.), *Family Poverty*, Duckworth, 1971, p. 99.
10 Ibid., p. 101.
11 For a critique of family income supplement see Barker, D., 'The Family income supplement', *New Society*, 5 August 1971 or Ch. 6 by the same writer in Bull, D. (ed.), op. cit. For a discussion of the administrative problems involved in implementing the scheme see Stacpoole, J., 'Running family income supplement', *New Society*, 13 January 1972.
12 Brown, C. and Dawson, D., *Personal Taxation Incentives and Tax Reform*, PEP, 1969.
13 The amount at present is 90p for the second child and £1 for each subsequent child.
14 Beveridge Report, p. 157.
15 *Proposals for a Tax Credit System*, HMSO, 1972.
16 Bosanquet, W., 'Banding poverty', *New Society*, 2 March 1972.
17 Carter, C., *Wealth*, Penguin, 1971, p. 122.
18 Walley, J., in Bull, D. (ed.), op. cit.
19 Bell, D., in Burns, E. (ed.), *Children's Allowances and the Economic Welfare of Children*, Citizens' Committee for Children of New York, 1968, p. 171.
20 Clegg, H., *How to Run an Incomes Policy*, Heinemann, 1971, p. 71.
21 For a discussion on income redistribution, see Saville, J., 'Labour and income re-distribution', *Socialist Register*, Merlin Press, 1965; Meade, J., *Efficiency, Equality and the Ownership of Property*, Allen & Unwin, 1964; Titmuss, R., *Income Distribution and Social Change*, Allen & Unwin, 1962.
22 Davis, K. and Moore, W., 'Some principles of stratification', *American Sociological Review*, vol. 10, No. 2, April 1945.

Notes

23 Tumin, M., 'Some principles of stratification: a critical analysis', *American Sociological Review*, vol. 18, No. 4, August 1953.
24 Wilcox, C., *Toward Social Welfare*, Irwin, 1969, p. 24.
25 Tawney, R., *Equality*, p. 113.
26 Crosland, A., *The Future of Socialism*, Cape, 1956, p. 149.
27 Wootton, B., *The Social Foundations of Wage Policy*, Allen & Unwin, 1962 ed., p. 162.
28 Rees, J., *Equality*, Macmillan, 1971, p. 122.
29 Crosland, A., op. cit., p. 150.
30 Parkin, F., *'Class Inequality and Political Order'*, MacGibbon & Kee, 1971, p. 123.
31 Galbraith, J., *The Affluent Society*, p. 73.

4 Unemployment and social security

1 Standing, G., 'Hidden workless', *New Society*, 14 October 1971; Preston, M., 'Unemployment: why we need a new measurement', *Lloyds Bank Review*, no. 104, April 1972.
2 Showler, B., 'Who are the unemployed?', *New Society*, 23 July 1970.
3 Sinfield, A., in Townsend, P. (ed.), *The Concept of Poverty*, Heinemann, 1970, p. 224.
4 Dorsey, J., in Eckstein, O. (ed.), *Studies in the Economics of Income Maintenance*, Brookings Institute, 1967, p. 231.
5 Medvin, N., 'Employment problems of older workers', *Social Security Bulletin*, vol. 20, no. 4, April 1957. Also Pym, D., *Industrial Society*, Penguin, 1968, Ch. 7.
6 Galbraith, J., *The New Industrial State*, Penguin, 1969, p. 246.
7 Sinfield, A., op. cit., p. 224.
8 Ministry of Labour 'Characteristics of the unemployed: 1964 Survey results', *Gazette*, April 1966.
9 Torode, J., 'The new unemployment?', *Guardian*, 18 January 1972.
10 Eisenberg, P. and Lazarfeld, P., 'The psychological effects of unemployment', *Psychological Bulletin*, 1938, pp. 358–90. For personal accounts of unemployed men, see Gould, T., 'Out of work', *New Society*, 20 May 1971.
11 Sinfield, A., op. cit., p. 227.
12 Daniel, W., 'Strategies for displaced persons', *Political and Economic Planning*, 1970, p. 9.
13 Tawney, R., *The Acquisitive Society*, Fontana, 1966, p. 41.
14 Rex, J., *Key Problems of Sociological Theory*, Routledge & Kegan Paul, 1961, p. 128.
15 Ibid., p. 129.
16 Galbraith, J., op. cit., p. 251.
17 Ibid., p. 252.

18 Kalecki, M., 'Political aspects of full employment', *Political Quarterly*, vol. 14, 1943.

19 Galbraith, J., op. cit., p. 247.

20 Gujarati, D., 'The behaviour of unemployment and unfilled vacancies in Great Britain, 1958–1971', *Economic Journal*, vol. 82, no. 325, March 1972.

21 Cairncross, F., 'Sinking in the jobless pool', *Observer*, 30 August 1970.

22 Dorsey, J., op. cit., p. 232.

23 Parker, S. R. et al., *Effects of the Redundancy Payments Act*, HMSO, 1971, p. 21.

24 Ibid., p. 13.

25 Hughes, J., 'Workers' control and the unemployed', *Spokesman*, no. 22, April-May 1972.

26 Day, A., 'Paving the road to prosperity', *Observer*, 23 March 1972.

27 Cairncross, F., 'Regions', *Observer*, 28 May 1972.

28 Zarka, C., 'Policies for promoting labour mobility in selected Western European countries', *International Labour Review*, vol. 95, no. 6, June 1967.

29 Brown, Barrat M., 'The causes of unemployment', *Spokesman*, no. 22, April-May 1972.

30 Jenkins, R., *What Matters Now*, Fontana, 1972, p. 30.

31 Daniel, W., op. cit., p. 47.

32 Shanks, M., *The Innovators*, Penguin, 1967, p. 249.

33 Kahn, H., *The Repercussions of Redundancy*, Allen & Unwin, 1964.

34 Reid, G., 'The role of the employment service in redeployment', *British Journal of Industrial Relations*, vol. 9, No. 2, 1971.

35 Department of Employment, *People and Jobs: a modern employment service*, HMSO, 1971.

36 'The job hunt', *New Society*, 16 December 1971.

37 Ibid.

38 Goldthorpe, J., Lockwood, D., et al., *The Affluent Worker in the Class Structure*, vol. 3, Cambridge University Press, 1969, p. 55.

39 Tawney, R., op. cit., Chs 7, 8 and 9.

40 Coates, K. and Topham, A., *Industrial Democracy in Great Britain*, MacGibbon & Kee, 1968.

41 Parker, S., *The Future of Work and Leisure*, Paladin, 1972, p. 131.

42 For a discussion of the administrative requirements for redundancy payments and unemployment benefits, see George, V., *Social Security: Beveridge and After*, Routledge & Kegan Paul, 1968, Ch. 5.

43 Parker, S. R., et al., op. cit., p. 7.

44 The maximum amount of a redundancy allowance is £1,200 though the average amount paid in 1971 was £264.

45 Kahn, H., op. cit., p. 232.

46 Wedderburn, D., in Pym, D. (ed.), op. cit., p. 72.

Notes

47 Sinfield, A., op. cit., p. 223.
48 Ibid., p. 224.
49 Lynes, T., 'Four weeks misrule', *New Society*, 20 January 1972.
50 Ministry of Social Security, *The Administration of the Wage Stop*, HMSO, 1967, p. 1.
51 Ibid., p. 2.
52 Wootton, B., *Remuneration in a Welfare State*, Eleanor Rathbone Memorial Lecture, Liverpool University Press, 1961, p. 14.
53 Sinfield, A., op. cit., p. 233.
54 The number of unemployment review officers who interview unemployed persons receiving supplementary benefit rose from 22 in December 1961, to 51 in December 1966, and to 117 in December 1971. *Poverty*, No. 20–1, Winter 1972, p. 23.
55 Ministry of Social Security, op. cit., p. 4.
56 Child Poverty Action Group, *The Administration of the Wage Stop*, London, 1972.
57 Ministry of Social Security, op. cit., p. 6.
58 Ibid., p. 12.
59 Ministry of Labour, *Gazette*, April 1962 and April 1964.
60 Goldthorpe, J. and Lockwood, D. *et al.*, *The Affluent Worker in the Class Structure*, Cambridge University Press, 1969, vol. 1.
61 Hill, M., 'Are the work-shy a myth?', *New Society*, 30 July 1970.

5 Old age and social security

1 Spengler, J., in Kreps, J. (ed.), *Employment, Income, and Retirement Problems of the Aged*, Duke University Press, 1963, p. 28.
2 Neugarten, B., in Becker, H. (ed.), *Social Problems: A Modern Approach*, Wiley, 1966, p. 168.
3 Orbach, H., in Tibbitts, C., and Donahue, W. (eds.), *Aging Around the World*, Columbia University Press, 1962, p. 54, for a discussion on the changes that led to the creation of the role of retirement.
4 Gerig, D., 'Pensionable age under old-age pension schemes', *International Labour Review*, vol. 72, 1964.
5 Pilcher, D., *et al.*, 'Some correlates of normal pensionable age', *International Social Security Review*, vol. 21, No. 3, 1968.
6 Neugarten, B., op. cit., p. 174.
7 Wedderburn, D., 'Economic aspects of ageing', *International Social Science Journal*, vol. 15, No. 3, 1963.
8 Piachaud, D., 'Supertaxing retirement', *New Society*, 15 July 1971.
9 ILO, *Introduction to Social Security*, Geneva, 1969, p. 78.
10 Townsend, P., *The Family Life of Old People*, Routledge & Kegan Paul, 1957; Loether, H., *Problems of Ageing*, Dickenson, California, 1967.
11 Shanas, E., Townsend, P. *et al.*, *Old People in Three Industrial Societies*, Routledge & Kegan Paul, 1968, p. 437.

12 Neugarten, B., op. cit., p. 193.
13 Ministry of Pensions and National Insurance, *Financial and Other Circumstances of Retirement Pensioners*, HMSO, 1966, Table III.1, p. 19.
14 Townsend, P., and Wedderburn, D., *The Aged in The Welfare State*, Bell, 1965.
15 Burns, E., *The American Social Security System*, Houghton Mifflin, 1951, p. 36.
16 Shanas, E., Townsend, P. *et al.*, op. cit., p. 411.
17 Ministry of Pensions and National Insurance, op. cit., Table II.4, p. 12.
18 Shanas, E., Townsend, P. *et al.*, op. cit., Table XII.13, p. 379.
19 *National Superannuation and Social Insurance*, Cmnd. 3883, HMSO, 1969 (proposals of the Labour government). *A Strategy for Pensions*, Cmnd. 4755, HMSO, 1971 (proposals of the Conservative government).
20 Lynes, T., *Labour's Pension Plan*, Fabian Tract 396, Fabian Society, 1969.
21 Heclo, H., 'Pension politics', *New Society*, 23 September 1971.

6 Social security and society

 1 Zollner, D., 'Relating social insurance benefits to earnings', *International Social Security Review*, Year 23, No. 2, 1970.
 2 Wynn, M., *Family Policy*, Michael Joseph, 1970, p. 24.
 3 Schorr, A., 'Filial responsibility and the aging, or beyond pluck and luck', *International Social Security Bulletin*, vol. 25, No. 5, May 1962.
 4 In 1970, fifteen such unemployed men were sent to prison. Department of Health and Social Security, *Annual Report*, Cmnd. 4714, HMSO, 1970, p. 89.
 5 George, V. and Wilding, P., *Motherless Families*, Routledge & Kegan Paul, 1972, pp. 198–208.
 6 Glass, D., *Population Policies and Movements in Europe*, Cass, 1940.
 7 Schorr, A., 'Income maintenance and the birth rate', *Social Security Bulletin*, vol. 28, No. 12, December 1965.
 8 Paukert, F., 'Social security and income redistribution', *International Labour Review*, vol. 98, No. 5, November 1968.
 9 Fisher, P., 'Social security and development planning: some issues', *Social Security Bulletin*, vol. 30, No. 6, June 1967.
10 Paukert, F., op. cit.,
11 Titmuss, R., *Commitment to Welfare*, Allen & Unwin, 1968, p. 133.
12 Eckstein, O. (ed.), *Studies in the Economics of Income Maintenance*, Brookings Institute, 1967; Burkus, J., 'Some aspects of income redistribution through social security in four Western European countries', *International Labour Review*, vol. 97, No. 2, February 1968.

13 Lampman, R., in Jenkins, S. (ed.), *Social Security in International Perspective*, Columbia University Press, 1969, pp. 29–35.

14 Huntford, R., *The New Totalitarians*, Allen Lane, 1971, p. 183.

15 Higuchi, T., 'The special treatment of employment injury in social security', *International Labour Review*, vol. 102, No. 2, August 1970.

16 Townsend, P., 'The disabled need help', *New Society*, 28 September 1967; Report of the Royal Commission of Inquiry, *Compensation for Personal Injury in New Zealand*, Government Printer, Wellington, 1967.

17 Tibergen, J. and Bouwmeesters, J., in Kassalow, E. (ed.), *The Role of Social Security in Economic Development*, U.S. Department of Health, Education and Welfare, 1968, p. 41.

18 Rimlinger, G., *Welfare Policy and Industrialization in Europe, America and Russia*, Wiley, 1971, p. 305.

19 Wolff, R. P., Barrington, Moore Jr, Marcuse, H., *A Critique of Pure Tolerance*, Beacon Press, 1965, p. 81.

20 Gerth, H. and Mills, C. W. (eds), *From Max Weber*, Oxford University Press, 1948, p. 128.

Bibliography

Official papers (published by HMSO)

Beveridge Report, see Inter-departmental Committee.

Central Statistical Office, *Social Trends*, No. 2, 1971.

Department of Employment, *People and Jobs: a modern employment service*, 1971.

Department of Employment and Productivity, *A National Minimum Wage*, 1969.

Department of Health and Social Security, *Annual Report*, 1970, Cmnd. 4714.

Government Actuary, *Occupational Pension Schemes*, First Survey, 1956; Second Survey, 1966; Third Survey, 1968.

Green Paper, *Proposals for a Tax Credit System*, 1972.

Inter-departmental Committee (Ministries of Health, Labour, Pensions etc.), *Social Insurance and Allied Services* (Beveridge Report), 1942, Cmd. 6404.

Ministry of Labour, 'Characteristics of the unemployed: 1964 Survey results', *Gazette*, April 1966.

Ministry of Labour and National Service, *Report of an Enquiry into Household Expenditure in 1953-4*, 1957.

Ministry of Pensions and National Insurance, *Financial and Other Circumstances of Retirement Pensioners*, 1966.

Ministry of Social Security, *The Administration of the Wage Stop*, 1967.

Ministry of Social Security, *Circumstances of Families*, 1967.

National Board for Prices and Incomes, *Productivity, Prices and Incomes Policy after 1969*, 1969, Cmnd. 4237.

National Board for Prices and Incomes, *General Problems of Low Pay*, 1971, Cmnd. 4648.

White Paper, *National Superannuation and Social Insurance* (proposals of the Labour government), 1969, Cmnd. 3883.

White Paper, *A Strategy for Pensions* (proposals of the Conservative government), 1971, Cmnd. 4755.

Books and articles

ABEL-SMITH, B. and TOWNSEND, P., *The Poor and the Poorest*, Bell, 1965.

ATKINSON, A., *Poverty in Britain and the Reform of Social Security*, Cambridge University Press, 1969.

ATKINSON, D., *Orthodox Consensus and Radical Alternative*, Heinemann, 1971.

BARKER, D., 'The family income supplement', *New Society*, 5 August 1971.
BECKER, H. (ed.), *Social Problems: A Modern Approach*, Wiley, 1966.
BELL, D., *The End of Ideology*, Free Press, 1960.
BENDIX, R., *Work and Authority in Industry*, Wiley, 1956.
BOSANQUET, W., 'Banding poverty', *New Society*, 2 March 1972.
BROWN, BARRAT, M., 'The causes of unemployment', *Spokesman*, No. 22, April-May 1972.
BROWN, C. and DAWSON, D., *Personal Taxation Incentives and Tax Reform*, PEP, 1969.
BULL, D. (ed.), *Family Poverty*, Duckworth, 1971.
BURKUS, J., 'Some aspects of income redistribution through social security in four Western European countries', *International Labour Review*, vol. 97, No. 2, February 1968.
BURNETT, J., *A History of the Cost of Living Index*, Penguin, 1969.
BURNS, E., *The American Social Security System*, Houghton Mifflin, 1951.
BURNS, E. (ed.), *Children's Allowances and the Economic Welfare of Children*, Citizens' Committee for Children of New York, 1968.
BUTLER, D. and ROSE, R., *The British General Election of 1959*, Macmillan, 1960.
CAIRNCROSS, F., 'Sinking in the jobless pool', *Observer*, 30 August 1970.
CAIRNCROSS, F., 'Regions', *Observer*, 28 May 1972.
CARTER, C., *Wealth*, Penguin, 1971.
CHILD POVERTY ACTION GROUP, *The Administration of the Wage Stop*, London, 1972.
CLEGG, H., *How to Run an Incomes Policy*, Heinemann, 1971.
COATES, K. and SILBURN, R., *Poverty: The Forgotten Englishmen*, Penguin, 1970.
COATES, K. and TOPHAM, A., *Industrial Democracy in Great Britain*, MacGibbon & Kee, 1968.
COHEN, P. S., *Modern Social Theory*, Heinemann, 1968.
COLE, D. and UTTING, J., *The Economic Circumstances of Old People*, Codicote, 1962.
COSER, L., 'The sociology of poverty', *Social Problems*, vol. 13, 1965.
CRAIG, F. W. S. (ed.), *British General Election Manifestos, 1918-1966*, Political Reference Publications, 1970.
CRIPPS, S., *Can Socialism Come by Constitutional Means?*, London, n.d.
CROSLAND, A., *The Future of Socialism*, Cape, 1956.
DANIEL, W., 'Strategies for displaced persons', *Political and Economic Planning*, 1970.
DAVIS, K. and MOORE, W., 'Some principles of stratification', *American Sociological Review*, vol. 10, No. 2, April 1945.
DAY, A., 'Paving the road to prosperity', *Observer*, 23 March 1972.
ECKSTEIN, O. (ed.), *Studies in the Economics of Income Maintenance*, Brookings Institute, 1967.

EISENBERG, P. and LAZARFELD, P., 'The psychological effects of unemployment', *Psychological Bulletin*, 1938.

FISHER, P., 'Social security and development planning: some issues', *Social Security Bulletin*, vol. 30, No. 6, June 1967.

GALBRAITH, J., *The Affluent Society*, Penguin, 1962.

GALBRAITH, J., *The New Industrial State*, Penguin, 1969.

GANS, H., *People and Plans*, Penguin, 1972.

GEORGE, V., *Social Security: Beveridge & After*, Routledge & Kegan Paul, 1968.

GEORGE, V. and WILDING, P., *Motherless Families*, Routledge & Kegan Paul, 1972.

GERIG, D., 'Pensionable age under old-age pension schemes', *International Labour Review*, vol. 72, 1964.

GERTH, H. and MILLS, C. W. (eds), *From Max Weber*, Oxford University Press, 1948.

GILBERT, B., *The Evolution of National Insurance in Great Britain*, Michael Joseph, 1966.

GILBERT, B., *British Social Policy, 1914–1939*, Batsford, 1970.

GLASS, D., *Population Policies and Movements in Europe*, Cass, London, 1940.

GOLDTHORPE, J., LOCKWOOD, D., *et al.*, *The Affluent Worker in the Class Structure*, Cambridge University Press, 1969.

GOULD, T., 'Out of work', *New Society*, 20 May 1971.

GRAY, B. K., *A History of English Philanthropy*, King, 1905.

GUJARATI, D., 'The behaviour of unemployment and unfilled vacancies in Great Britain, 1958–1971', *Economic Journal*, vol. 82, No. 325, March 1972.

HECLO, H., 'Pension politics', *New Society*, 23 September 1971.

HIGUCHI, T., 'The special treatment of employment injury in social security', *International Labour Review*, vol. 102, No. 2, August 1970.

HILL, M., 'Are the work-shy a myth?', *New Society*, 30 July 1970.

HOROWITZ, D., 'One-dimensional society', *International Socialist Journal*, Year 4, No. 24, December 1967.

HUGHES, J., 'Workers' control and the unemployed', *Spokesman*, No. 22, April-May 1972.

HUNTFORD, R., *The New Totalitarians*, Allen Lane, 1971.

ILO, *Introduction to Social Security*, Geneva, 1969.

JENKINS, R., *What Matters Now*, Fontana, 1972.

JENKINS, S. (ed.), *Social Security in International Perspective*, Columbia University Press, 1969.

JORDAN, W. K., *Philanthropy in England, 1480–1660*, Allen & Unwin, 1959.

KAHN, H., *The Repercussions of Redundancy*, Allen & Unwin, 1964.

KALECKI, M., 'Political aspects of full employment', *Political Quarterly*, vol. 14, 1943.

Bibliography

KASSALOW, E. (ed.), *The Role of Social Security in Economic Development*, U.S. Department of Health, Education and Welfare, 1968.

KREPS, J. (ed.), *Employment, Income, and Retirement Problems of the Aged*, Duke University Press, 1963.

LEWIS, O., *The Children of Sanchez*, Secker & Warburg, 1962.

LOETHER, H., *Problems of Ageing*, Dickenson, California, 1967.

LYNES, T., *National Assistance and National Prosperity*, Codicote, 1962.

LYNES, T., *Labour's Pension Plan*, Fabian Tract 396, Fabian Society, 1969.

LYNES, T., 'Four weeks misrule', *New Society*, 20 January 1972.

MCGREGOR, O. R., 'Social research and social policy in the nineteenth century', *British Journal of Sociology*, vol. 8, No. 1, March, 1957.

MARCUSE, H., *One-Dimensional Man*, Sphere Books, 1968.

MARRIS, P., *Widows and Their Families*, Routledge & Kegan Paul, 1958.

MARSDEN, D., Review of *Culture and Poverty: critique and counter-proposals*, by C. A. Valentine, Chicago University Press, 1968, in *Poverty*, No. 11, Summer 1969.

MARWICK, A., 'The Labour Party and the Welfare State in Britain, 1900–1948', *American Historical Review*, vol. 73, 1967.

MEADE, J., *Efficiency, Equality and the Ownership of Property*, Allen & Unwin, 1964.

MEDVIN, N., 'Employment problems of older workers', *Social Security Bulletin*, vol. 20, No. 4, April 1957.

MEISSNER, H. (ed.), *Poverty in the Affluent Society*, Harper & Row, 1966.

MILIBAND, R., *Parliamentary Socialism*, Allen & Unwin, 1961.

MILIBAND, R., *The State in Capitalist Society*, Weidenfeld & Nicolson, 1969.

ORSHANSKY, M., 'Counting the poor: another look at the poverty profile', *Social Security Bulletin*, 28, No. 1, January 1965.

PARKER, S., *The Future of Work and Leisure*, Paladin, 1972.

PARKER, S. R. et al., *Effects of the Redundancy Payments Act*, HMSO, 1971.

PARKIN, F., *Class Inequality and Political Order*, MacGibbon & Kee, London, 1971.

PAUKERT, F., 'Social security and income redistribution', *International Labour Review*, vol. 98, No. 5, November 1968.

PIACHAUD, D., 'Supertaxing retirement', *New Society*, 15 July 1971.

PILCHER, D. et al., 'Some correlates of normal pensionable age', *International Social Security Review*, vol. 21, No. 3, 1968.

PINKER, R., *Social Theory and Social Policy*, Heinemann, 1971.

PRESTON, M., 'Unemployment: why we need a new measurement', *Lloyds Bank Review*, no. 104, April 1972.

PYM, D., *Industrial Society*, Penguin, 1968.

REES, J., *Equality*, Macmillan, 1971.

REID, G., 'The role of the employment service in redeployment', *British Journal of Industrial Relations*, vol. 9, No. 2, 1971.

REX, J., *Key Problems in Sociological Theory*, Routledge & Kegan Paul, 1961.

RHYS, V., 'The sociology of social security', *Bulletin of the International Social Security Association*, Nos. 1–2, 1962.

RIMLINGER, G. V., *Welfare Policy and Industrialization in Europe, America and Russia*, Wiley, 1971.

ROACH, J. and ROACH, J. (eds), *Poverty*, Penguin, 1972.

ROSE, M., *The Relief of Poverty 1834–1914*, Macmillan, 1972.

ROWNTREE, B. S., *Poverty: A Study of Town Life*, Macmillan, 1901.

ROWNTREE, B. S., *Poverty and Progress: A Second Social Survey of York*, Longmans, 1941.

ROWNTREE, B. S. and LAVERS, G. R., *Poverty and the Welfare State*, Longmans, 1951.

Royal Commission, *Report on the Poor Laws*, 1834.

Royal Commission of Inquiry, *Compensation for Personal Injury in New Zealand*, report, New Zealand Government Printer, Wellington, 1967.

SAVILLE, J., 'Labour and income re-distribution', *Socialist Register*, Merlin Press, 1965.

SAVILLE, J., 'Labourism and the Labour Government', *Socialist Register*, Merlin Press, 1967.

SCHORR, A., 'Filial responsibility and the aging, or beyond pluck and luck', *International Social Security Bulletin*, vol. 25, No. 5, May 1962.

SCHORR, A., 'Income maintenance and the birth rate', *Social Security Bulletin*, vol. 28, No. 12, December 1965.

SCHWEINITZ, K. de, *England's Road to Social Security*, University of Pennsylvania Press, 1961.

SELIGMAN, B. (ed.), *Poverty as a Public Issue*, Free Press, 1965.

SHANAS, E., TOWNSEND, P., et al., *Old People in Three Industrial Societies*, Routledge & Kegan Paul, 1968.

SHANKS, M., *The Innovators*, Penguin, 1967.

SHERIDAN, G., 'Women, cheap labour', *Guardian*, 4 February 1972.

SHOWLER, B., 'Who are the unemployed?', *New Society*, 23 July 1970.

SMITH, A., *The Wealth of Nations*, 1776.

STACPOOLE, J., 'Running family income supplement', *New Society*, 13 January 1972.

STANDING, G., 'Hidden workless', *New Society*, 14 October 1971.

TAWNEY, R. H., *Religion and the Rise of Capitalism*, Penguin, 1948.

TAWNEY, R. H., *Equality*, Allen & Unwin, 1964.

TAWNEY, R. H., *The Acquisitive Society*, Fontana, 1966.

THOMPSON, E. P., *The Making of the English Working Class*, Penguin, 1968.

TIBBITTS, C. and DONAHUE, W. (eds), *Aging Around the World*, Columbia University Press, 1962.

TIMMS, N., *A Sociological Approach to Social Problems*, Routledge & Kegan Paul, 1967.

TITMUSS, R. M., *Income Distribution and Social Change*, Allen & Unwin, 1962.

TITMUSS, R. M., *Essays on the Welfare State*, Allen & Unwin, 1963.

TITMUSS, R. M., *Commitment to Welfare*, Allen & Unwin, 1968.

TORODE, J., 'The new unemployment?', *Guardian*, 18 January 1972.

TOWNSEND, P., *The Family Life of Old People*, Routledge & Kegan Paul, 1957.

TOWNSEND, P., 'The meaning of poverty', *British Journal of Sociology*, vol. 13, 1962.

TOWNSEND, P., 'The disabled need help', *New Society*, 28 September 1967.

TOWNSEND, P., *Poverty, Socialism and Labour in Power*, Fabian Tract 371, Fabian Society, 1967.

TOWNSEND, P. (ed.), *The Concept of Poverty*, Heinemann, 1970.

TOWNSEND, P. and WEDDERBURN, D. *The Aged in the Welfare State*, Bell, 1965.

TUMIN, M., 'Some principles of stratification: a critical analysis', *American Sociological Review*, vol. 18, No. 4, August 1953.

VALENTINE, C. A., *Culture and Poverty: critique and counter-proposals*, Chicago University Press, 1968.

WEBB. B., *My Apprenticeship*, Longmans, Green, 1926

WEBB, S. and B., *English Poor Law History*, Longmans, Green, 1927, vol. I.

WEDDERBURN, D., 'Economic aspects of ageing', *International Social Science Journal*, vol. 15, No. 3, 1963.

WILCOX, C., *Toward Social Welfare*, Irwin, 1969.

WOLFF, R. P., BARRINGTON, MOORE JR and MARCUSE, H., *A Critique of Pure Tolerance*, Beacon Press, 1965.

WOOTTON, B., *Remuneration in a Welfare State*, Eleanor Rathbone Memorial Lecture, Liverpool University Press, 1961.

WOOTTON, B., *The Social Foundations of Wage Policy*, Allen & Unwin, 1962.

WYNN, M., *Family Policy*, Michael Joseph, 1970.

YOUNG, M. (ed.), *Forecasting in the Social Sciences*, Heinemann, 1968.

ZARKA, C., 'Policies for promoting labour mobility in selected Western European countries', *International Labour Review*, Vol. 95, No. 6, June 1967.

ZÖLLNER, D., 'Relating social insurance benefits to earnings', *International Social Security Review*, vol. 23, no. 2, 1970.

Name index

Subject Index

Alms giving, 3
Assimilation, 2
Authority, 2, 12–13

Beveridge Report, 23–4, 47–8, 71,
   102, 104, 112

Child Poverty Action Group, 105,
   106
Child tax allowances, 69–70
Church, 4, 5
Civil War, 6
Conflict
   inequality, 73–8
   social class, 2
   unemployment, 85–7
Conservative Party, 23, 30, 32,
   91, 92, 119–23

Deterrence, 12, 67–8

Earnings-related benefits, 32–3,
   51–2
Enclosure movement, 9
End of ideology, 29–32
Enfranchisement, 13–14

Family
   filial responsibility, 125–8
   insurance benefits, 124–5
   one-parent, 126
Family allowances, 69–71, 73
Family income supplement, 67–9,
   72
Feudalism, 3, 4
Filial responsibility, 125–8

General Strike (1926), 21

Humanitarianism, 14–15

Ideology, 2, 3, 37–8, 48, 66, 68,
   70–1, 104–5

Individualism, 10, 56, 78
Industrial training, 96–7
Inequality, 40–1, 68, 73–8, 120–1
Insurance benefits, level of, 48–52
Insurance principle, 17–18, 33–4,
   35, 36

Labour Party, 19–22, 23, 25–6,
   30, 32, 91, 119–23
Laissez-faire, 7–8
Less eligibility, 12, 71, 104
Liberal Party, 17
Low pay
   abolition, 78–9
   characteristics, 61–2
   extent, 58–61
   minimum wage, 71–2
   poverty, 53
   supplementary benefit, 62–3

Marxism, 14, 18, 31–2
Minimum wage, 11, 64–6, 71–2

National Assistance Board, 26,
   34, 53

Occupational benefits, 27, 118,
   119–20
Old age
   demographic data, 109
   economic circumstances, 114–18
   employment, 110–13
   pensions, 16–17, 19
   retirement age, 109–10
   role of retirement, 114

Poverty
   as ascribed status, 3–4
   causes, 53–4
   Church, 4
   culture, 39–40
   definition, 40
   economic prosperity, 26–7

153